James Sidney Jones

The Geisha

A Story of a Tea House

James Sidney Jones

The Geisha
A Story of a Tea House

ISBN/EAN: 9783337172268

Printed in Europe, USA, Canada, Australia, Japan

Cover: Foto ©Thomas Meinert / pixelio.de

More available books at **www.hansebooks.com**

A Japanese Musical Play

IN TWO ACTS

LIBRETTO BY
OWEN HALL.

LYRICS BY
HARRY GREENBANK.

MUSIC BY
SIDNEY JONES.

Authors of "An Artist's Model" and "A Gaiety Girl."

VOCAL SCORE		6s. net.
Do.	(Bound in Cloth)	10s. „
PIANOFORTE SOLO		3s. „
LYRICS		6d. „

London

HOPWOOD & CREW, 42, NEW BOND STREET, W.

Boston, New York, and Chicago: The White-Smith Music Publishing Company.

Sole Agents for Germany and Austria: Messrs. Bote & Bock.

Copyright 1896 by Hopwood & Crew.

All performing Rights in this Opera are reserved. Single detached numbers may be sung at Concerts, not more than two at one Concert, but they must be given without Stage Costume or Action. In no case must such performance be announced as a "Selection" from the Opera. Application for right of performing the above Opera must be made to Mr. GEORGE EDWARDES, Daly's Theatre, London.

Performed at Daly's Theatre, London.

Dramatis Personæ.

O Mimosa San ... ... (Chief Geisha)	Miss Marie Tempest.
Juliette Diamant ... (A French Girl, attached to Tea House as Interpreter) ...	Miss Juliette Nesville.
Nami (Wave of the Sea) ... ... (an Attendant)	Miss Kristine Yudall.
O Kiku San (Chrysanthemum)		Miss Emelie Herve.
O Hana San (Blossom) ...		Miss Mary Fawcett.
O Kinkoto San (Golden Harp)	(Geisha)	Miss Elise Cooke.
Komurasaki San (Little Violet)		Miss Mary Collette.
Lady Constance Wynne (an English Visitor in Japan, travelling in her Yacht) ...	Miss Maud Hobson.
Miss Marie Worthington ...		Miss Blanche Massey.
Miss Ethel Hurst ...	(English Ladies, Guests of Lady	Miss Hetty Hamer.
Miss Mabel Grant ...	Constance)	Miss Alice Davis.
Miss Louie Plumpton ...		Miss Margaret Fraser.
Miss Molly Seamore ...		Miss Letty Lind.
Reginald Fairfax		Mr. Hayden Coffin.
Dick Cunningham		Mr. Louis Bradfield
Arthur Cuddy ...	(Officers of H.M.S. "The Turtle")	Mr. Leedham Bantock.
George Grimston		Mr. Sydney Ellison.
Tommy Stanley (Midshipman)		Miss Lydia Flopp
Captain Katana ...	(Captain of the Governor's Guard)	Mr. William Philp.
Takemine	(Sergeant of the Governor's Guard)	Mr. Fredk. Rosse.
Wun-hi ... ... (a Chinaman ; proprietor of Tea House) ...	Mr. Huntley Wright.
The Marquis Imari ...(Chief of Police and Governor of the Province) ...	Mr. Harry Monkhouse

Coolies, Attendants. Mousmés, Guards, &c.

ACT I.—*The Tea House of Ten Thousand Joys.* ACT II.—*A Chrysanthemum Fête in the Palace Gardens.*

Time—The present.

The action of the play takes place in Japan outside the Treaty Limits.

CONTENTS.

Act I.

"THE GEISHA."

(A STORY OF A TEA HOUSE.)

A JAPANESE MUSICAL PLAY.

WORDS BY	LYRICS BY	MUSIC BY
OWEN HALL.	HARRY GREENBANK.	SIDNEY JONES.

N.º 1. OPENING CHORUS— "HAPPY JAPAN."

Allegro moderato.

PIANO.

Here we hast - en pit ter

Here we hast - en pit ter

Dawns the day in East - ern sky ....

Dawns the day in East - ern sky ....

pat - ter .... Where the ti - ny tea - cups clat - ter;

pat - ter .... Where the ti - ny tea - cups clat - ter;

.... Mounts the

.... Mounts the

Shad_ed from his fu ry heat_ed......
Shad_ed from his fu - ry heat_ed......
gold - en Sun - God high ....
gold - en Sun - God high ....
.... Still at tea you find us seat_ed;
.... Still at tea you find us seat_ed;
.... Pass - es
.... Pass - es

4

tea un _ til to _ mor _ row No more tea .... un _

No more tea .... un _

No more tea .... un _

No more tea .... un

_ til to _ mor _ _ row......................

_ til to _ mor _ row......................

_ til to _ mor _ _ row......................

_ til to _ mor _ _ row......................

cresc.

Hap_py Ja _ pan, Gar _ den of glit _ ter! Flow_er and fan
Hap_py Ja pan, Gar _ den of glit _ ter! Flow_er and fan
Hap_py Ja pan, Gar _ den of glit _ ter! Flow_er and fan
Hap_py Ja _ pan, Gar _ den of glit _ ter! Flow_er and fan
f
Flut _ ter and flit _ ter; Land of bam _ boo, (Ju _ ve_nile whacker)
Flut _ ter and flit _ ter; Land of bam _ boo, (Ju _ ve_nile whacker)
Flut _ ter and flit _ ter; Land of bam _ boo, (Ju _ ve_nile whacker)
Flut _ ter and flit _ ter; Land of bam _ boo, (Ju _ ve_nile whacker)

Por - ce - lain too, Tea - tray and lac - quer. Hap - py Ja - pan,

Por - ce - lain too, Tea - tray and lac - quer. Hap - py Ja - pan,

Por - ce - lain too, Tea - tray and lac - quer. Hap - py Ja - pan,

Por - ce - lain too, Tea - tray and lac - quer. Hap - py Ja - pan,

Allegretto.

Hap - py Ja - pan.

Hap - py Ja - pan.

Hap - py Ja - pan.

Hap - py Ja - pan.

8

Shall we sing you while they bring you Tea or cof_fee, Sirs, Dain_ty ly_ric

Shall we sing you while they bring you Tea or cof_fee, Sirs, Dain_ty ly_ric

pan _ e _ gyr _ ic Of the gen_tle _ men We've a so_lo touch_ing po_lo

pan _ e _ gyr _ ic Of the gen_tle men We've a so_lo touch_ing po_lo

For the of _ fi _ cers And a ron_do rather fond, O sent_ i _ men_tal men.

For the of _ fi _ cers And a ron_do rather fond, O sent _ i _ men_tal men.

Of a hymn in praise of wo_men Are you fan_ci _ ers,   Or a son_net

Of a hymn in praise of wo_men Are you fan_ci _ ers,   Or a son_net

to a bon_net Su_per_cil_i _ ous?   We've a dit_ty of the ci_ty

to a bon_net Su_per_cil_i _ ous?   We've a dit_ty of the ci_ty

For fi _ nan_ci _ ers And a bal_lad of a sa_lad For the bilious!

For fi _ nan_ci _ ers And a bal_lad of a sa_lad For the bilious!

Mer - ry lit - tle geis - ha we! Come a - long at once and see
Mer - ry lit - tle geis - ha we! Come a - long at once and see
Am - ple en - ter - tainment free, Giv - en as you take your tea,
Am - ple en - ter - tainment free, Giv - en as you take your tea,
CHORUS.
Charm - ing lit - tle geis - ha they! Come a - long and hear them play;
Charm - ing lit - tle geis - ha they! Come a - long and hear them play;
Charm - ing lit - tle geis - ha they! Come a - long and hear them play;
Charm - ing lit - tle geis - ha they! Come a - long and hear them play;

All of it is free they say No_thing in the world to pay

All of it is free they say No_thing in the world to pay.

All of it is free they say No_thing in the world to pay

All of it is free they say No_thing in the world to pay.

All of it is free, they say, and no_thing in the world to

All of it is free, they say, and no_thing in the world to

All of it is free, they say, and no_thing in the world to

All of it is free, they say, and no_thing in the world to

Tempo I.
pay .... Hap_py Ja _ pan, Gar_den of glit_ter!
pay .... Hap_py Ja _ pan, Gar_den of glit_ter!
pay .... Hap_py Ja _ pan, Gar_den of glit_ter!
pay .... Hap_py Ja _ pan, Gar_den of glit_ter!
Tempo I.
ff
Flow_er and fan Flut_ter and flit_ter; Land of bam_boo,
Flow_er and fan Flut_ter and flit_ter; Land of bam_boo,
Flow_er and fan Flut_ter and flit_ter; Land of bam_boo,
Flow_er and fan Flut_ter and flit_ter; Land of bam_boo,

(Ju_ve_nile whacker) Por_ce_lain too, Tea-tray and lac_quer!

(Ju_ve_nile whacker) Por_ce_lain too, Tea-tray and lac_quer!

(Ju_ve_nile whacker) Por_ce_lain too, Tea-tray and lac_quer!

(Ju_ve_nile whacker) Por_ce_lain too, Tea-tray and lac_quer!

Hap_py Ja_pan, Hap_py Ja_pan, Hap_py Ja_pan.

Hap_py Ja_pan, Hap_py Ja_pan, Hap_py Ja_pan.

Hap_py Ja_pan, Hap_py Ja_pan, Hap_py Ja_pan.

Hap_py Ja_pan, Hap_py Ja_pan, Hap_py Ja_pan.

Nº 2. ENTRANCE OF OFFICERS.— "HERE THEY COME."

Allegro.

PIANO.

Here they come! Oh look and see! Great big Eng_lish sai _ lor men!

Here they come! Oh look and see! Great big Eng_lish sai _ lor men!

Here they come! Oh look and see! Great big Eng_lish sai _ lor men!

Here they come! Oh look and see! Great big Eng_lish sai _ lor men!

Eng - lish.man he likes our tea. Comes to taste it now and then.

Eng - lish.man he likes our tea. Comes to taste it now and then.

Eng - lish.man he likes our tea, Comes to taste it now and then.

Eng - lish.man he likes our tea, Comes to taste it now and then.

Great big sai . lors walk like this— Fight with a . ny man they please,

Great big sai . lors walk like this— Fight with a . ny man they please,

Mar_ry lit _ tle Eng_lish miss, Flirt with pret_ty Ja _ pan _ ese ....

Mar_ry lit _ tle Eng_lish miss, Flirt with pret_ty Ja _ pan _ ese ....

Here they come! Oh, look and see!

Here they come! Oh, look and see!

Here they come! Oh, look and see!

Here they come! Oh, look and see!

Great big English sai_lor men! Eng_lish_man he likes our tea, Comes to taste it

Great big English sai_lor men! Eng_lish_man he likes our tea, Comes to taste it

Great big English sai_lor men! Eng_lish_man he likes our tea, Comes to taste it

Great big English sai_lor men! Eng_lish_man he likes our tea, Comes to taste it

now and then, Comes to taste it now and then, yes, now and then.

now and then, Comes to taste it now and then, yes, now and then.

now and then, Comes to taste it now and then, yes, now and then

now and then, Comes to taste it now and then, yes, now and then.

FAIRFAX.

Though you've seen a good deal in your

walks a _ bout, Here's the pret _ ti _ est place of the lot! — It's the tea house that ev'_ry-one talks a_bout— A de_light_ful_ly cu_ri_ous spot.

CUNNINCHAM.

Are your stories a myth and a mock_e_ry Of the ex_cel_lent tea that they bring, Of the quaint lit_tle pie_ces of crock_e_ry, And the gay lit_tle gei_sha who sing?

Oh we've heard of the frolic and fun Of those dear lit_tle Ja_pan_ese
1st OFFICER.
Oh we've heard of the frolic and fun Of those dear lit_tle Ja_pan_ese
2nd OFFICER.
Oh we've heard of the frolic and fun Of those dear lit_tle Ja_pan_ese
3rd OFFICER.
Oh we've heard of the frolic and fun Of those dear lit_tle Ja_pan_ese
elves, So we thought the best thing to be done Was to come here and see for our_
elves, So we thought the best thing to be done Was to come here and see for our_
elves, So we thought the best thing to be done Was to come here and see for our_
elves, So we thought the best thing to be done Was to come here and see for our_

CHORUS.

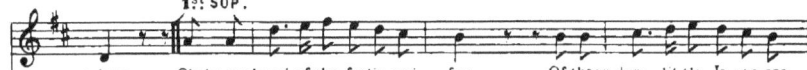

_ selves   Oh they've heard of the frolic and   fun   Of those dear lit_tle Ja_pan_ese

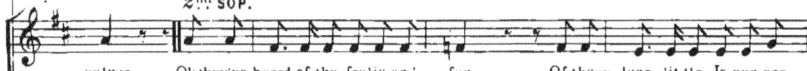

_ selves   Oh they've heard of the frolic and   fun   Of those dear lit_tle Ja_pan_ese

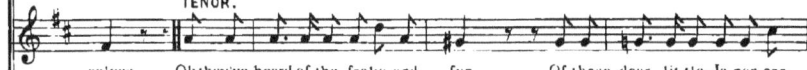

_ selves   Oh they've heard of the frolic and   fun   Of those dear lit_tle Ja_pan_ese

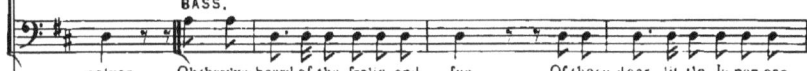

_ selves   Oh they've heard of the frolic and   fun   Of those dear lit_tle Ja_pan_ese

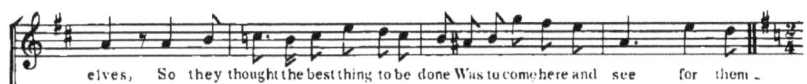

elves,   So they thought the best thing to be done Was to come here and   see   for   them _

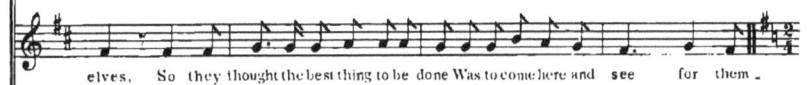

elves,   So they thought the best thing to be done Was to come here and   see   for   them _

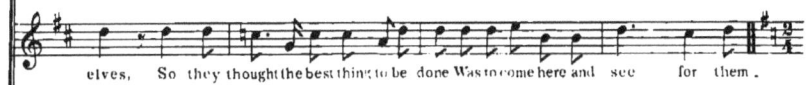

elves,   So they thought the best thing to be done Was to come here and   see   for   them _

elves,   So they thought the best thing to be done Was to come here and   see   for   them _

selves.

selves.

selves.

selves.

_ff_

Though your ways are queer and fun _ ny, Japs are ve _ ry glad you've come.

Though your ways are queer and fun _ ny, Japs are ve _ ry glad you've come.

Though your ways are queer and fun _ ny, Japs are ve _ ry glad you've come.

Though your ways are queer and fun _ ny, Japs are ve _ ry glad you've come.

Eng _ lish_man has lots of mo _ ney. Eng _ lish_man will spare us some
Eng _ lish_man has lots of mo _ ney, Eng _ lish_man will spare us some.
Eng _ lish_man has lots of mo _ ney, Eng _ lish_man will spare us some,
Eng _ lish_man has lots of mo _ ney, Eng _ lish_man will spare us some,
Pret _ ty geis_ha will a _ muse, Dance or song she won't re _ fuse.
Pret _ ty geis_ha will a _ muse, Dance or song she won't re _ fuse.
Pret _ ty geis_ha will a _ muse, Dance or song she won't re _ fuse.
Pret _ ty geis_ha will a _ muse, Dance or song she won't re _ fuse.

Great big Eng_lish sai_lors, please. Try our tea_pot Jap_an_ese,
Great big Eng_lish sai_lors, please. Try our tea_pot Jap_an_ese,
Great big Eng_lish sai_lors, please. Try our tea_pot Jap_an_ese,
Great big Eng_lish sai_lors, please, Try our tea_pot Jap_an_ese,
Sai_lors please oh try our tea_pot Jap_an_ese.
Sai_lors please oh try our tea_pot Jap_an_ese.
Sai_lors please oh try our tea_pot Jap_an_ese.
Sai_lors please oh try our tea_pot Jap_an_ese.
pp
dim.
pp
8va
dim.

Nº 3. SONG.— (FAIRFAX & OFFICERS.)"JACK'S THE BOY."

COMPOSED BY
LIONEL MONCKTON.

Allegro moderato.

PIANO.

Of all the lads that be There is on_ly one for me. And his
When Jack has got his pay He's the gay_est of the gay. For the

home is on the waters deep and blue:.......... But a friend he'll ne_ver lack, For the
mo_ney in his pocket burns a hole:.......... And he's ne _ ver happy quite Till he's

world's in love with Jack—He's the smartest and the best of fel_lows too!.......... So his
spent it left and right—Like a jo _ vi_al and careless hearted soul.......... Tho' he's

hand we like to grip As he goes a_board his ship, While the
ve _ ry far from shy When a pret _ ty girl is by, Yet a
p
girls are fit to break their pret _ ty hearts. For he
lad may sure _ ly "kiss and ne _ ver tell!" And when
cres. rall - - en -
loves them by the score When he gai _ ly comes a_shore, And they're
du _ ty calls him back. Taut and trim goes Jol _ ly Jack To the
cres. rall - - en -
- f tan - - - do rit.
sad when their Jack de - parts!
ship that he loves so well!
- f tan - - - do
dim.e rit.

Jack's the boy for work! Jack's the boy for play! Jack's the lad. When girls are sad, To kiss the tears a_way! Ah! . Hard as nails - afloat; best of friends ashore; Jack a_hoy! You're just the boy That all our hearts adore! all our hearts adore! all our hearts a_dore! all our hearts a_dore!

No 4. SONG— (CUNNINGHAM.) "THE DEAR LITTLE JAPPY-JAP-JAPPY."

Moderato.

PIANO.

CUN.

1. There came to the land of Ja _ _ _ pan —. . . . . To the
2. They walk'd in the shade of the trees. . . . . In the
3. So Jack has de _ _ part _ _ ed in doubt. . . . . From that

CUN.

sea _ port of fair Na _ ga _ _ sa _ ki. . . . . . From an is _ land a _ far Such a
gar _ dens of fair Na _ ga _ _ sa _ ki. . . . . . And her cheeks they were pink At the
mai _ den of fair Na _ ga _ _ sa _ ki! . . . . . Though he wept and he sigh'd At the

CUN.

jol _ ly Jack Tar, With his horn _ pipe, his grog and his bac _ cy. . . . . Now it
nau _ ti _ _ cal wink, And the ma _ ri _ time man _ ners of Jac _ ky! . . . . Though the
loss of a bride Till the cap _ tain and crew thought him crac _ ky. . . . . And he

CUN.

chanc'd that he pick'd up a fan...... For a dear lit-tle Ja-pan-ese
tar could-n't speak Ja-pan-ese,...... Yet in Eng-lish he ask'd her to
vows, as he cruis-es a-bout.....(Though by les-sons and books as a

CUN.

par-ty,.... And he turn'd her young head When he gal-lant-ly said, "You're a
mar-ry;... Then she crept to his side, And her fan o-pen'd wide, As she
rule bored).. That all sea-men A.B.s Should be taught Ja-pan-ese By a

CUN.

trim lit-tle ves-sel my hear-ty!" So that dear lit-tle Jap-py-Jap-
mur-mur'd,"Hai!Ku-shi-ko-mu-ri!" But he knew not a scrap-py-scrap-
ra-ther too li-be-ral School Board! But that dear lit-tle Jap-py-Jap-

CUN.

Jap-py..... Set her smart lit-tle cap-py-cap-cap-py..... At the
scrap-py..... Of the lan-guage of Jap-py-Jap-Jap-py!.... Had she
Jap-py,.... She has fill'd up the gap-py-gap-gap-py..... And has

CUN.

jol - ly Jack Tar From the is - land a - far In the west of the map - py - map -
told him to go — With a Ja - pan-ese "No!"— Or with "Yes!" made him hap - py - hap -
cho - sen in - stead To be hap - pi - ly wed To a Ja - pan - ese chap - py - chap -

GEISHA.

CUN.

map - py! So that dear lit - tle Jap - py - Jap - Jap - py . . . . . Set her
hap - py? But he knew not a scrap - py - scrap - scrap - py . . . . . Of the
chap - py! But that dear lit - tle Jap - py - Jap - Jap - py . . . . . She has

CUNNINGHAM.

GEI.

smart lit - tle cap - py - cap - cap - py . . . . At the jol - ly Jack Tar From the
lan - guage of Jap - py - Jap - Jap - py! . . . . Had she told him to go — With a
fill'd up the gap - py - gap - gap - py, ... And has cho - sen in - stead To be

(ALL TOGETHER.)

CUN.

is - land a - far In the west of the map - py - map - map - py!
Ja - pan - ese "No!"— Or with "Yes!" made him hap - py - hap - hap - py?
hap - pi - ly wed To a Ja - pan - ese chap - py - chap - chap - py!

D.C.

DANCE (after third verse.)

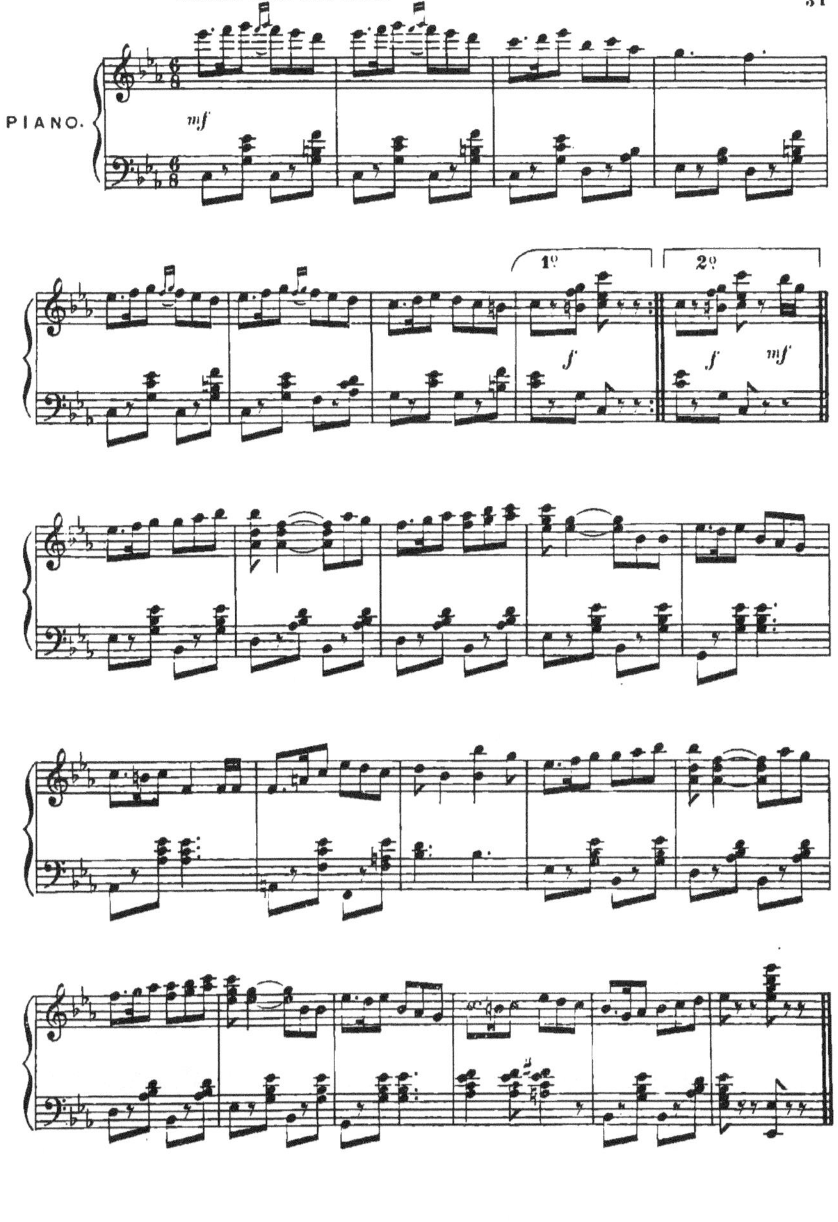

No. 5. SONG.—"THE AMOROUS GOLDFISH."

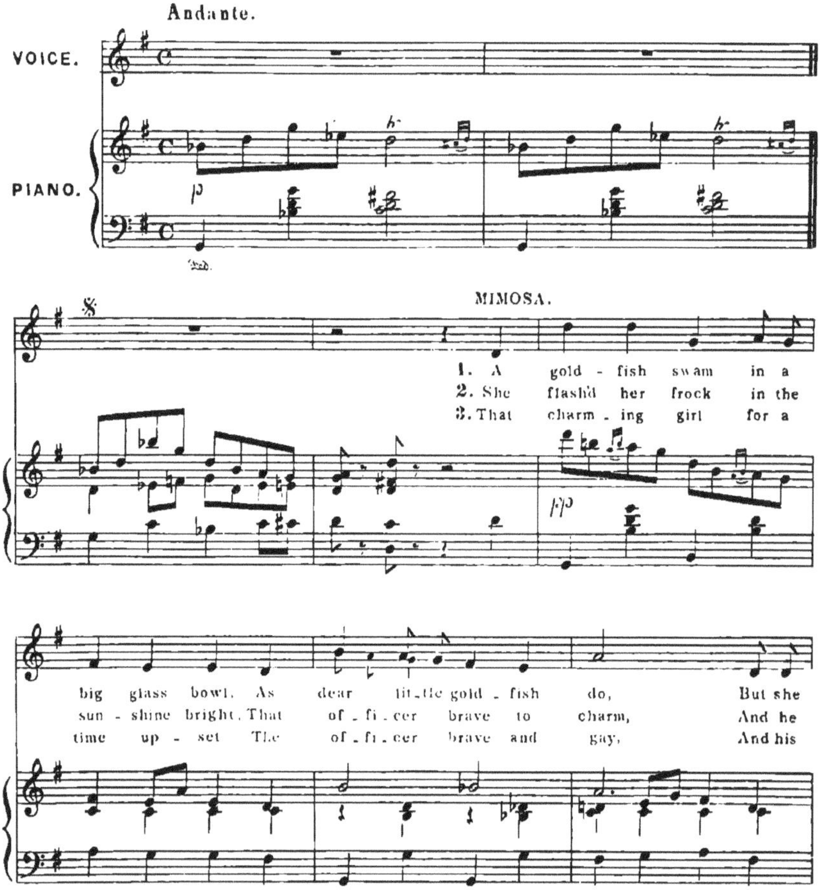

loved with the whole of her heart and soul An of-fi-cer brave from the
vowed she was quite a de-light-ful sight. So her spirits were gay till he
sad lit-tle pet he con-trived to for-get. For with never a crumb did he

o - cean wave, And she thought that he loved her too! Her
came one day With a girl on his stal-wart arm! In
chance to come, So the gold-fish pined a - way! Un -

small in - side he dai - ly fed With crumbs of the best di -
whis - pers low they talked of love He begged for a rose and a
- til at last some care - less soul, With a smash knock'd o - ver the

gest - ive bread, "This kind at - ten - tion proves," said she, "How ex -
worn out glove; But when they kissed a fond good-bye, The
big glass bowl, And there on the car - pet, dead and cold, Lay the

34

ceed-ing-ly fond he is of me!".
poor lit-tl-gold - fish longed to die.
poor lit-tle fish in her frock of gold!

And she thought"It's fit _ fit _ fit _ ter... He should
And she sobbed"It's bit _ bit _ bit _ ter... He should
But her fate so bit _ bit _ bit _ ter... Is a

love my glit _ glit _ glit _ ter... Than his heart give a _ way To the
love this crit _ crit _ crit _ ter... When I thought he would wish For a
sto _ ry fit _ fit _ fit _ ter... For a sad lit _ tle sigh And a

but-ter-flies gay, Or the birds that twit _ twit twit _ ter."
nice lit-tle fish With a frock all glit _ glit glit _ ter."
tear in the eye Than a thought_less tit _ tit _ tit _ ter!

D.C.

No. 6. KISSING DUET.— (MIMOSA & FAIRFAX.)

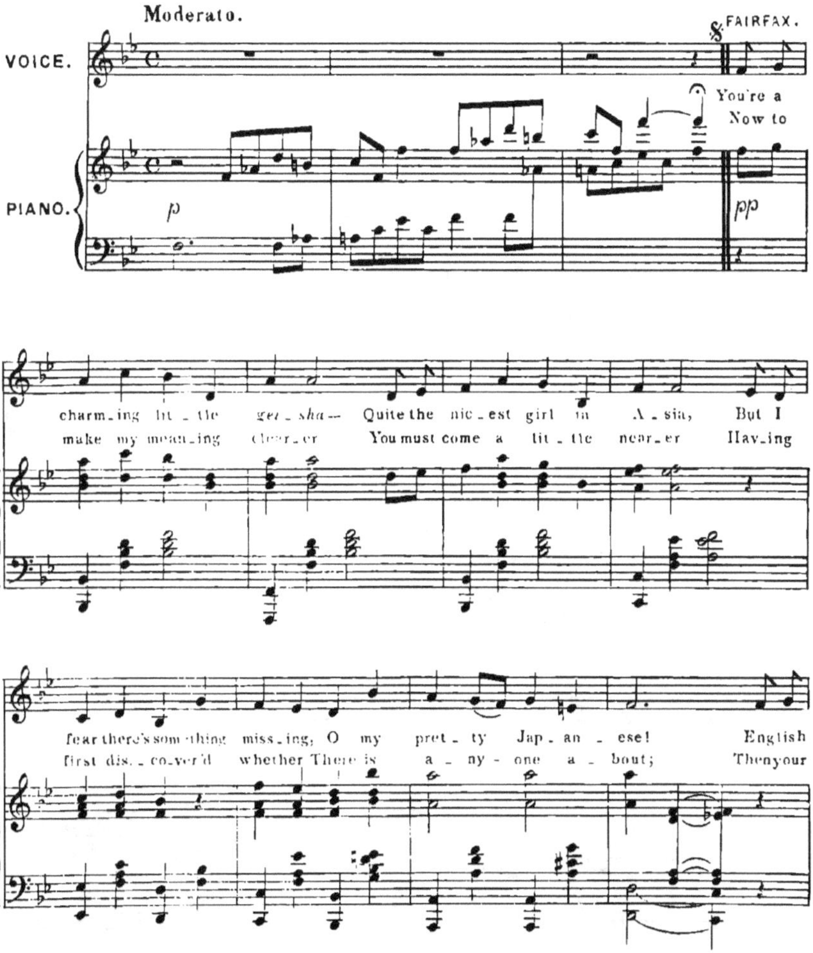

36

French and Ger_man miss_es Do not ask me what a kiss is— They are
face half-shy_ly rais_ing Till your eyes in *his* are gaz_ing, Place your

MIMOSA.   *più mosso*

all ex_perts at kiss_ing. Will you teach me, if you please? I be
pret_ty lips to_ge_ther In a dain_ty lit_tle pout.(MIM)If a

più mosso

_love I'm quick and cle_ver, And I pro_mise I'll en_dea_vour In the
smile my cheeks should dim_ple, It's be_cause it's all so sim_ple! Why of

task to do you cre_dit If your pu_pil I may be! O my
such a tame pro_ceed_ing Should you make so great a fuss? It's a

accell.
sai - lor bright and breez - y, Is it dif - fi - cult or ea - sy? - Is it
farce ab - surd - ly hol - low - But per - haps there's more to fol - low? For in -
accell.
FAIRFAX.
nice - or shall I dread it? On - ly wait and you shall see!
- struc - tion I am plead - ing! - And I give it to you - thus! (Kisses her.)
poco rall.
Ped:
MIMOSA.
a tempo poco meno mosso.
FAIRFAX.
I am half a - fraid to try - Then the task we won't pur -
It has charms I can't ex - plain - Which you ne - ver knew be -
rall.
a tempo poco meno mosso.
MIMOSA.
FAIRFAX.
- sue. Shall I like it by - and - by? It's ob - ject - ed to by few!
- fore! Teach me once, just once a - gain! Pret - ty pu - pils I a - dore.
pp

MIMOSA. *Più mosso.*

FAIRFAX.

Lit _ tle mai _ den. Won _ der - la _ den, Ev' _ ry
Lit _ tle mai _ den. Won _ der - la _ den, Ev' _ ry

Lit _ tle mai _ den, Won _ der - la _ den, Ev' _ ry
Lit _ tle mai _ den, Won _ der - la _ den, Ev' _ ry

Più mosso.

M

day learns some _ thing new.
day learns some _ thing more.

F

day learns some _ thing new.
day learns some _ thing more. *Presto.*

Nº 7. CONCERTED PIECE — "IF YOU WILL COME TO TEA."

GEISHA.

If you will come to tea, Sir

One and Two and Three, We'll do our best For an

Eng _ lish guest On an A _ si _ at _ ic spree. We'll

dance and sing for you Our re _ _ per _ _ to _ _ _ ry

through, And show you then, You of _ fi _ cer _ men, What

smart lit _ tle girls can do . . . .

. . . What smart lit _ tle girls can do ! . . . .

For you're all so bright and breezy – O! That we're sure to find it ea-sy – O! To
tease 'e O! And please 'e O! With our an-tics Jap-an-ese-y O!
OFFICERS.
We are

To tease 'e O! And
To tease 'e O! And
To tease 'e O! And
sai_lors bright and bree_zy O! And we're sure to find it ea_sy O! To tease 'e O! And
sai_lors bright and bree_zy O! And we're sure to find it ea_sy O! To tease 'e O! And
sai_lors bright and bree_zy O! And we're sure to find it ea_sy O! To tease 'e O! And
please 'e O! With our antics Jap_an_ese_y, With our antics Japan_ese_y O! . . . .
please 'e O! With our antics Jap_an_ese_y, With our antics Japan_ese_y O! . . . .
please 'e O! With our antics Jap_an_ese_y, With our antics Japan_ese_y O! . . . .
please 'e O! With your antics Jap_an_ese_y, With your antics Japan_ese_y O! . . . .
please 'e O! With your antics Jap_an_ese_y, With your antics Japan_ese_y O! . . . .
please 'e O! With your antics Jap_an_ese_y, With your antics Japan_ese_y O! . . . .

OFFICERS.

Of course we'll come in _ side, For none of us have tried How dance and song With a fine Souchong Are ef _ fec _ tive _ ly al _ _ lied. But if you've spo _ ken true, We'll quick _ ly prove to you What sai_lors three Of the Queen's Na_vee For good lit_tle girls will do........

.... For good lit_tle girls will do.

We are sai_lors bright and bree_zy O! So of

We are sai_lors bright and bree_zy O! So of

We are sai_lors bright and bree_zy O! So of

course we find it ea __ sy O! To tease 'e O! And

course we find it ea __ sy O! To tease 'e O! And

course we find it ea __ sy O! To tease 'e O! And

For you're

For you're

For you're

squeeze 'e O! Lit __ tle Mis __ sy Jap __ an __ ese __ y O! . . . . . .

squeeze 'e O! Lit __ tle Mis __ sy Jap __ an __ ese __ y O! . . . . . .

squeeze 'e O! Lit __ tle Mis __ sy Jap __ an __ ese __ y O! . . . . . .

all so bright and bree_zy O! That we're sure to find it ea_sy O! To
all so bright and bree_zy O! That we're sure to find it ea_sy O! To
all so bright and bree_zy O! That we're sure to find it ea_sy O! To
To
To
To
tease 'e O! And please 'e O! With our an_tics Jap_an__ese_y, With our
tease 'e O! And please 'e O! With our an_tics Jap_an__ese_y, With our
tease 'e O! And please 'e O! With our an_tics Jap_an__ese_y, With our
tease 'e O! And squeeze 'e O! Lit_tle Mis_sy Jap_an__ese_y, Lit_tle
tease 'e O! And squeeze 'e O! Lit_tle Mis_sy Jap_an__ese_y, Lit_tle
tease 'e O! And squeeze 'e O! Lit_tle Mis_sy Jap_an__ese_y, Lit_tle

an - tics Jap - an - ese - - - y O! . . . .
an - tics Jap - an - ese - - - y O! . . . .
an - tics Jap - an - ese - - - y O! . . . .
Mis - sy Jap - an - ese - - - y O . . . .
Mis - sy Jap - an - ese - - - y O! . . . .
Mis - sy Jap - an - ese - - - y O! . . . .
DANCE.
pp
cresc:
f

Nº 8. CHORUS OF LAMENTATION.

Lento.

PIANO.

p

CHORUS.

p

Oh, will they sell our mas-ter up, Or take him off to gaol, And

p

Oh, will they sell our mas-ter up, Or take him off to gaol, And

p

Oh, will they sell our mas-ter up, Or take him off to gaol, And

p

Oh, will they sell our mas-ter up, Or take him off to gaol, And

dim:

on the tea-house plaster up The no-ti-ces of sale? What_

on the tea-house plaster up The no_ti_ces of sale? What_

on the tea-house plaster up The no_ti_ces of sale? What_

on the tea-house plaster up The no_ti_ces of sale? What_e_ver

_e_ver will be_come of us If this should come to pass? It's

_e_ver will be-come of us If this should come to pass? It's

_e_ver will be_come of us If this should come to pass? It's

will be_come of us If this should come to pass? It's

bound to ru - in some of us! A - las, a - las, a - las, a -

bound to ru - in some of us! A - las, a - las, a - las, a -

bound to ru - in some of us! A - las, a - las, a - las, a -

bound to ru - in some of us! A - las, a - las, a - las, a -

- las, a - - las, a - las, a - - las!

- las, a - - las, a - las, a - - las!

- las, a - - las, a - las, a - - las!

- las, a - - las, a - las, a - - las!

GEISHA (sobbing.)
Here's a dreadful blow, oh, oh! Fill - ing us with woe, oh, oh!
Here's a dreadful blow, oh, oh! Fill - ing us with woe, oh, oh!
How could Geisha know oh, oh! Fate would treat them so? oh, oh!
How could Geisha know oh, oh! Fate would treat them so? oh, oh!
Pret - ty fa - ces show Tears that fast - er flow.
Pret - ty fa - ces show Tears that fast - er flow.
Oh, oh! Oh, oh!
Oh, oh! Oh, oh!
Oh, oh! Oh, oh!
Oh, oh! Oh, oh!

Please at pri _ ces low, Do not let us go, Oh,
Please at pri _ ces low, Do not let us go, Oh,
Oh, oh! Oh,
Oh, oh! Oh,
Oh, oh! Oh,
Oh, oh! Oh,
oh! Here's a dreadful blow, oh, oh! Fill _ ing us with
oh! Here's a dreadful blow, oh, oh! Fill _ ing us with
oh! Here's a dreadful blow, oh, oh! Fill _ ing us with
oh! Here's a dreadful blow, oh, oh! Fill _ ing us with
oh! Here's a dreadful blow, oh, oh! Fill _ ing us with
oh! Here's a dreadful blow, oh, oh! Fill _ ing us with

woe, oh, oh! How could Gei-sha know oh, oh! Fate would treat them

so, oh, oh! What-ev-er will be-come of us, If this should come to

54

pass? It's bound to ru_in some of us, A_ _ las, a _ las, a-

pass? It's bound to ru_in some of us, A_ _ las, a _ las, a-

pass? It's bound to ru _ in some of us, A_ _ las, a _ las, a-

pass? It's bound to ru_in some of us, A_ _ las, a _ las, a-

pass? It's bound to ru_in some of us, A_ _ las, a _ las, a-

pass? It's bound to ru _ in some of us, A_ _ las, a _ las, a-

_ las!

_ las!

_ las!

_ las!

_ las!

_ las!

dim:

№ 9. CONCERTED PIECE—"WE'RE GOING TO CALL ON THE MARQUIS."

(FAIRFAX.) This in-fa-mous lord Shall have his re-ward My
(OFFICERS.) You'll par-don us, pray, For ask-ing the way, Our

an-ger each mo-ment in-crea - - ses! Let's qui-et-ly slip A-
ig-no-rance kind-ly for-giv - - -ing, But oh! we are so Im-

-way to our ship, And blow the old beg-gar to pie - - ces.(GUN.)Of
-pa-tient to know Where Mis-ter I-ma-ri is liv - - -ing.(CEI.)We'll

course to bom - bard A fel - low's back yard Is jol - ly good fun, but you'll
show you the road To reach his a - bode, De - - light - ed your fa - vour at

rue it! You'd bet - ter in - stead Try punching his head. (GIRLS.)We'd
earn - ing. Sim - pli - ci - ty quite, Keep well to the right, And

like to be there while you do it!
care - ful - ly look for a turn - ing.

pp   cresc:

ALL.

We're

pp

ff   pp

ALL.
go_ing to call on the Mar_ _quis To pay off a nice lit_tle score And
ALL.
won't he be chat_ty When rat_a_tat tat_ty We knock at his dig_ni_fied door? We've
ALL.
something to say to the Mar_ _quis, It's something too funny to miss, For
ALL.
af_ter pooh-poohing All how-do-you-doing We're go_ing to say it like this!–
1º
D.C.

2º CHORUS.

We're go-ing to call on the Mar-quis To pay off a nice lit-tle score, And

We're go-ing to call on the Mar-quis To pay off a nice lit-tle score, And

We're go-ing to call on the Mar-quis To pay off a nice lit-tle score, And

We're go-ing to call on the Mar-quis To pay off a nice lit-tle score, And

won't he be chat-ty When rat - a - tat-tat-ty We knock at his dig-ni-fied door. We've

won't he be chat-ty When rat - a - tat-tat-ty We knock at his dig-ni-fied door. We've

won't he be chat-ty When rat - a - tat-tat-ty We knock at his dig-ni-fied door. We've

won't he be chat-ty When rat - a - tat-tat-ty We knock at his dig-ni-fied door. We've something to say to the Mar _ quis, It's something too fun_ny to miss For

something to say to the Mar _ quis, It's something too fun_ny to miss For

something to say to the Mar _ quis, It's something too fun_ny to miss For

something to say to the Mar _ quis, It's something too fun_ny to miss For

af_ter pooh-poohing All how-do-you-do_ing We're go_ing to say it like this!

af_ter pooh-poohing All how-do-you-do_ing We're go_ing to say it like this!

af_ter pooh-poohing All how-do-you-do_ing We're go_ing to say it like this!

af_ter pooh-poohing All how-do-you-do_ing go_ing to say it like this!

N.º *10.* TOY DUET.— (MOLLY & FAIRFAX.)

Allegretto.

PIANO.

(MOLLY.) When I was but a ti — — ny tot My
(FAIR.) I knew I had a fa — — mous top, A
(MOLLY.) What jol — — ly games I used to play With

dol — lies were a love — — ly lot, For one — a la — — dy
paint — ed gun that used to pop, A spot — ted horse that
lit — tle boys a — — cross the way! We rac'd and romp'd as

born and bred— Could shut her eyes and.. move her head. "Pa —
boast — ed legs Ex — — act — — ly like four wood — en pegs; But
chil — dren d — I gave them backs at... leap — frog too. We

_pa!" "Ma _ _ ma!" an _ _ o _ ther talk'd, And when you wound her..
though I own'd a... box of bricks, And crim _ son mon _ _ keys
bowl'd our hoops and.. flew our kites, At hop _ scotch had some

up she walk'd, But more than a _ ny... o _ ther toy I
climb _ ing sticks, My in _ fant joys were cen _ tred in A
splen _ did fights; But life was on _ _ ly quite com _ plete With

loved a lit _ _ tle drum _ mer boy. (FAIR.) Of course I know the
nod _ ding Chi _ nese Man _ da _ rin. (MOLLY.) Of course I know the
Punch and Ju _ dy in the street. (FAIR.) How well it's va _ _ ried

sort.. you mean— That drum _ mer boy I've of _ _ ten seen.
sort.. you mean— That Man _ da _ rin I've of _ _ ten seen.
charms I know— I've seen that Punch and Ju _ _ dy show!

(MOLLY.) For he
(FLIR.) For his
(MOLLY.) Mis - ter

beats a fee - - ble rum - ti - tum - tum When he hits his lit - - tle
bells will tin - - kle ring - a - ding-ding, While his head he'll grave - - ly
Punch comes up with root - i - toot - toot. To the ba - - by he's a

drum - ti - tum - tum, And his arms seem ra - - ther numb - ti - tum - tum As they
swing - a - ding-ding, And his hands to - - ge - - ther bring - a - ding-ding When you
brute - i - toot - toot; But his Tu - - by makes him hoot - i - toot - toot, And the

BOTH.

rise and down _ ward come - ti - tum - tum. Oh, the dear old
pull a piece of *string-a-ding-ding.* Oh, the dear old
bea _ dle bids him *scoot - i - toot - toot.* Oh, the dear old

toys, ... and the sim _ _ ple ways..... Of those
toys, ... and the sim _ _ ple ways..... Of those
games, ... and the sim _ _ ple ways..... Of those

child _ _ ish - ver _ se _ ry, Might - be - wor _ se _ ry, Sweet _ ly cur _ so _ ry
child _ _ ish - ver _ se _ ry, Might - be - wor _ se _ ry, Sweet _ ly cur _ so _ ry
child _ _ ish - ver _ se _ ry, Might - be - wor _ se _ ry, Sweet _ ly cur _ so _ ry

Nur _ se _ ry Days!
Nur _ se _ ry Days!
Nur _ se _ ry Days!

f

D.C.

Nº 11. SONG — (MIMOSA.) "A GEISHA'S LIFE."

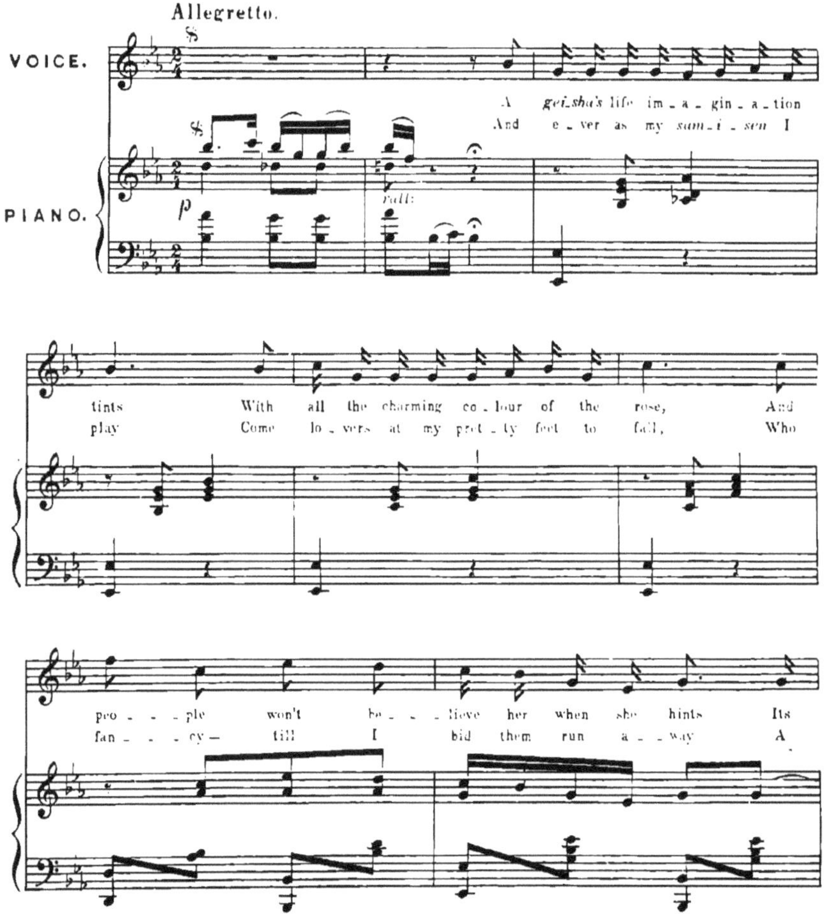

beauties are not quite what they sup_pose. Be _ cause I'm ra-ther quaint and pictur_
_geisha's heart has room e _ nough for all! Yet Love may work his will, if so he

_ esque, They think that for a but_ter_fly like me Ex _
please; His ma_ gic can a woman's heart un _ lock As

_ is_tence is de _ light _ ful _ ly grotesque— How ve_ry much mis _ ta _ ken folks may
well be_ neath ki _ mo _ no Jap_ an_ ese As un_ der a _ ny smart Pa _ ris _ ian

Tempo di Valse.

be!
frock.

"Oh, dance, my lit — tle gei – sha gay, And sing your... pret – ty
"We love you, lit — tle gei – sha gay! Oh, won't you... love us

songs!" they say; But don't you see It's hard on me Who
too?" they say; But don't you see It's lost on me Who

sing and dance the live – long day?. "Oh, dance........ and
hear the same thing day by day?.

sing.......... your pret – ty songs!" they say;........ But

don't you see It's hard on me Who sing the live long day?.. sing the

live long day......... Who sing

Nº 12. RECITATIVE.— ATTENTION PRAY.

Allegretto.

VOICE.

TAKAMINI.

At-ten-tion, pray! and si-lence, if you

PIANO.

please! The Tea House Reg-u-la-tion Act de-crees

By Section Seven-teen, Sub-section Three That if a

hold-er of a licence be Found guil-ty af-ter tri-al or be-fore—

Of dis_o_bedience to su_pe_ri_or Au_tho_ri_ty;

By this en_act_ment old, His Tea-house and its

contents must be sold; And all in_dentures of his *geisha* too, By

IMARI.

public auction— un_reserv'd—must go! Such is the law! It is! I

70

TAKAMINI.

made it so! My

du_ty I must now pro_ceed to do.

ad lib. a tempo.
Lot number one! Bring forth Mim_o_sa San, The champion

geish_a, pride of all Ja_pan!

CHORUS.

Come forth, Mim _ o _ sa— Pride of all Ja_

Come forth, Mim _ o _ sa— Pride of all Ja_

Come forth, Mim _ o _ sa— Pride of all Ja_

Come forth, Mim _ o _ sa— Pride of all Ja_

KATANA.

_pan, Queen of the Tea-house, O Mim_n_sa San! Oh,

_pan,..... Queen of the Tea-house, O Mim_n_sa San!

_pan, Queen of the Tea-house, O Mim_n_sa San!

_pan,..... Queen of the Tea-house, O Mim_n_sa San!

help me, comrade, ere it is too late, To save Mimo _ sa from this dreadful

FAIRFAX.

fate! Stop! If your country you would not dis-

_grace, ... Give orders that this sale shall not take place! Come,

_men, what code of honor do you hold? — Will you stand by and see a woman sold?

Nº 12ª SONG.— (FAIRFAX & CHORUS.) "CHIVALRY."

FAIRFAX.

While na_ture with man_hood en_
No mat_ter what na_tion may

_dows us And beau_ty our pul_ses can fire, There's
claim us Or un_der what flag we par_ade, A

ne_ver a sight that can rouse us Like
mo_ment's in_ac_tion would shame us When

wo_man in dan_ger most dire. We
wo_man has need of our aid. The

ask not the why or the where _ fore, The
ve _ ri _ est out _ cast and strang _ er Ap _

wrong or the right of her cause— When
_ peals to our sym pa _ thies then; E

man has a wo _ man to dare for, Her
_ nough that a wo _ man's in dan _ ger— E _

weak _ ness and need are his laws! O
_ nough that she's plead _ ing to men! O

Poco meno mosso.

men, by the hearts that are in us; By chivalry, honour and right, The

wrongs of a woman must win us Till death in her service to fight!

CHORUS.

O men, by the hearts that are in you, By chivalry, honour and

O men, by the hearts that are in you, By chivalry, honour and

O men, by the hearts that are in us, By chivalry, honour and

O men, by the hearts that are in us, By chivalry, honour and

f

rall.
right, The wrongs of a wo_man must win you, Till death in her ser_vice to
right, The wrongs of a wo_man must win you, Till death in her ser_vice to
right, The wrongs of a wo_man must win us, Till death in her ser_vice to
right, The wrongs of a wo_man must win us, Till death in her ser_vice to
1º
2º
fight! fight!..........................
fight! fight!..........................
fight! fight!..........................
fight! fight!..........................
D. C.

Nº 13. SONG — (MOLLY & CHORUS.) "CHON KINA."

PIANO.

M.

1. I'm the smart_est lit_tle *gei-sha* in Ja _ pan, ... And the
2. Please to no_tice how cor_rect and high_ly bred . . . . . . Is the
3. I'm con _ si_der'd quite an O _ ri _ en _ tal belle, ... And they

M.

peo _ ple call me Ro _ li Po _ li Sun— . . . . Lost in
hair e _ rect _ ed stiff _ ly on my head, ... All se _
tell me I per _ form ex _ treme _ ly well . . . . On _ the

M.

ad _ _ mi _ ra _ tion ut _ ter At the va _ _ rie _ ga _ ted flut _ ter Of my
_vere _ _ ly coil'd and braid _ ed, While my cheeks are pink _ ly sha _ ded, And my
su _ _ mi _ sen or *ko _ to*—While my ve _ _ ry la _ test pho _ to In an

M.

cle _ _ ver _ ly ma _ ni _ pu _ la _ ted fan. . . . . I can
lips are tint _ ed e _ _ le _ gant _ ly red! . . . . I'm a
ar _ _ ti _ cle that's al _ ways sure to sell. . . . . When they

M.

dance to a _ _ ny mea _ sure that is gay, ... To and
vo _ _ ta _ _ ry of fa _ shion as it flies, ... And my
dal _ _ ly o _ _ ver dain _ _ ty cups of tea—. . . . . The at

M.

fro in dream _ y fa _ shion I can sway, ... And if
la _ test new *ki _ mo _ no* will sur _ _ prise; . . . . But the
_trac _ tions of the *cha _ ya* come to see—. . . . . Rich and

still my art en-ti-ces Then at ex-tra spe-cial pri-ces I can
charms of Ro-li Po-li Will not cap-ti-vate you whol-ly Till you
haugh-ty, poor and low-ly Call for pret-ty Ro-li Po-li Ev'ry

dance for you in *quite an-o-ther* way. . . . .
gaze in-to her li-quid al-mond eyes. . . . .
cus-to-mer is sure to or-der me! . . . .

Chon ki-na, chon ki-na. Chon chon. ki-na ki-na,

Na-ga-sa-ki, Yo-ko-hu-ma. Ha-ko-da-te hoi!

80

CHORUS.

1st SOPRANO.

Chon ki_na, chon ki_na, Chon chon, ki_na ki_na,

2nd SOPRANO.

Chon ki_na, chon ki_na, Chon chon, ki_na ki_na,

TENOR.

Chon ki_na, chon ki_na, Chon chon, ki_na ki_na,

BASS.

Chon ki_na, chon ki_na, Chon chon, ki_na ki_na,

p

Na_ga_sa_ki, Yo_ko_ha_ma, Ha_ko_da_te hoi!

Na_ga_sa_ki, Yo_ko_ha_ma, Ha_ko_da_te hoi!

Na_ga_sa_ki, Yo_ko_ha_ma, Ha_ko_da_te hoi!

Na_ga_sa_ki, Yo_ko_ha_ma, Ha_ko_da_te hoi!

ff

ff

D.C.

(*After third verse.*)

Ki - ri - gi - ri - - su hoi!

Ki - ri - gi - ri - - su hoi!

Ki - ri - gi - ri - - su hoi!

Ki - ri - gi - ri - - su hoi!

Ki - ri - gi - ri - su hoi!

Ki - ri - gi - ri - su hoi!

Ki - ri - gi - ri - su hoi!

Ki - ri - gi - ri - su hoi!

DANCE.

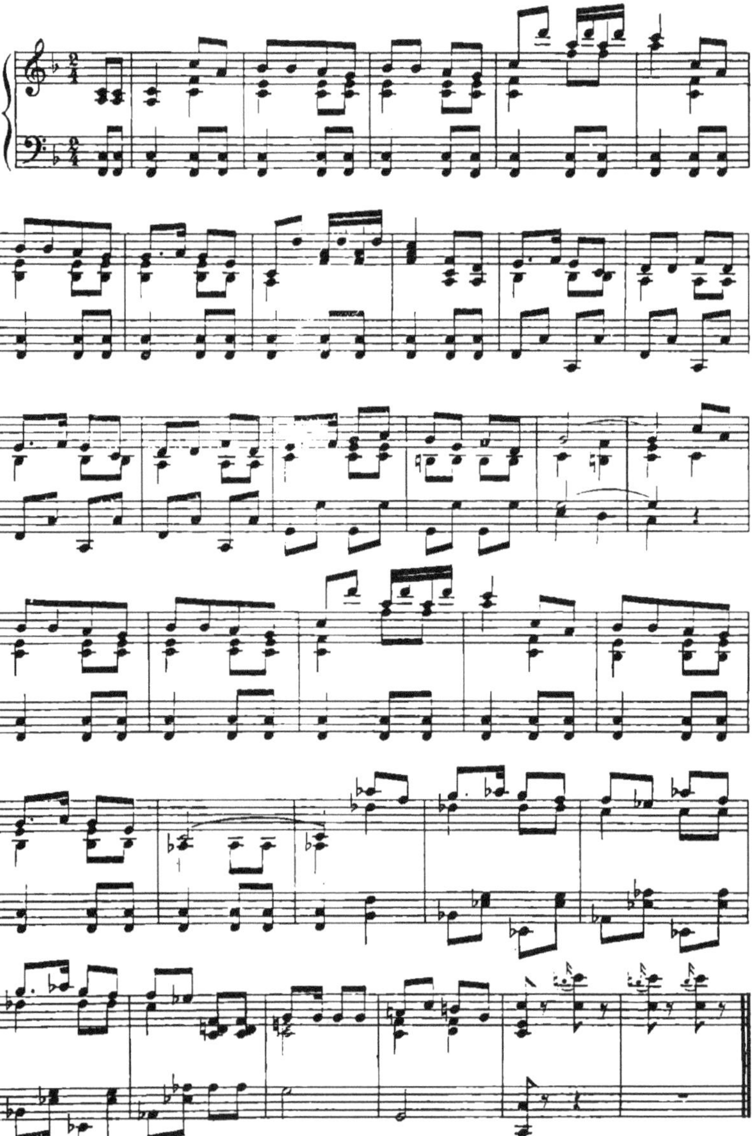

pp>

Chon ki _ na, chon ki _ na, Chon chon, ki _ na ki _ na,

pp>

Chon ki _ na, chon ki _ na, Chon chon, ki _ na ki _ na,

pp>

Chon ki _ na, chon ki _ na. Chon chon, ki _ na ki _ na,

pp>

Chon ki _ na, chon ki _ na, Chon chon, ki _ na ki _ na,

pp

Na _ _ ga _ sa _ ki, Yo _ ko _ ha _ ma, Ha _ ko _ da _ té hoï!

Na _ _ ga _ sa _ ki, Yo _ ko _ ha _ ma, Ha _ ko _ da _ té hoï!

Na _ _ ga _ sa _ ki, Yo _ ko _ ha _ ma, Ha _ ko _ da _ té hoï!

Na _ _ ga _ sa _ ki, Yo _ ko _ ha _ ma, Ha _ ko _ da _ té hoï!

ff
Chon ki - na, chon ki - na, Chon chon, ki - na ki - na,
Chon ki - na, chon ki - na, Chon chon, ki - na ki - na,
Chon ki - na, chon ki - na, Chon chon, ki - na ki - na,
Chon ki - na, chon ki - na, Chon chon, ki - na ki - na,
Na - ga - sa - ki, Yo - ko - ha - ma, Ha - ko - da - té hoi!
Na - ga - sa - ki, Yo - ko - ha - ma, Ha - ko - da - té hoi!
Na - ga - sa - ki, Yo - ko - ha - ma, Ha - ko - da - té hoi!
Na - ga - sa - ki, Yo - ko - ha - ma, Ha - ko - da - té hoi!

№14. FINALE. ACT I — "THOUGH OF STAYING TOO LONG."

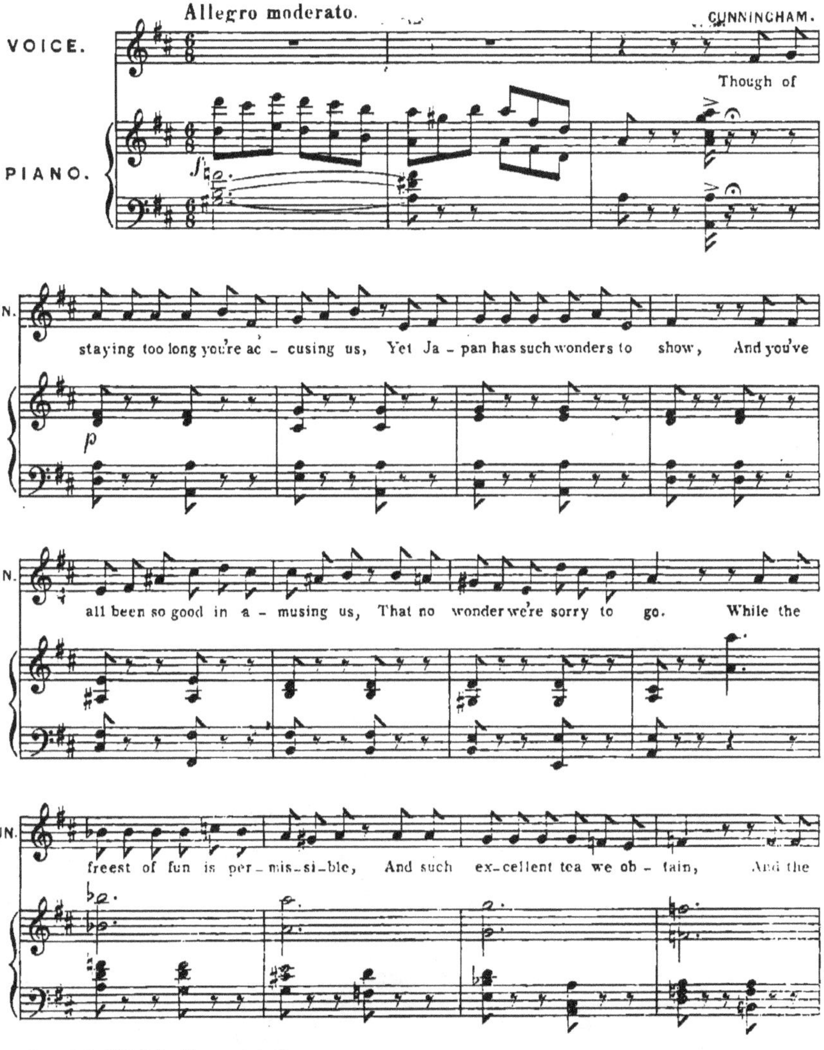

CUN.
girls are so quaint and so kiss-a-ble, We shall cer-tain-ly come here a - gain! . . . .
CUN.
OFFICERS.
. . . For to pass the most pleasant of days You should always contrive when you
For to pass the most pleasant of days You should always contrive when you
For to pass the most pleasant of days You should always contrive when you
can To at - ten-tively study the ways Of the dear lit-tle girls of Ja -
can To at - ten-tively study the ways Of the dear lit-tle girls of Ja -
can To at - ten-tively study the ways Of the dear lit-tle girls of Ja -

CHORUS.

1st SOP.

Yes to pass the most pleasant of days You should always contrive when you can To at _

2nd SOP.

_pan. Yes to pass the most pleasant of days You should always contrive when you can To at _

TENOR.

_pan. Yes to pass the most pleasant of days You should always contrive when you can To at _

BASS.

_pan. Yes to pass the most pleasant of days You should always contrive when you can To at _

f

_tentively study the ways Of the dear little girls of Ja_pan.

_tentively study the ways Of the dear little girls of Ja_pan.

_tentively study the ways Of the dear little girls of Ja_pan.

tentively study the ways Of the dear little girls of Ja_pan.

rall:

p

CHORUS.

Night ap-proaches clear and star-ry— Silver shadows soft-ly fall, Bring-ing rest to great I-ma-ri, Wel-come rest to one and all.

KATANA.

Pearl of the ra_diant Eastern sea, Light of a sol_dier's life,

Time in its course will set thee free— Free to be_come my wife!

All that my heart de_sires to say Would that my lips could tell;

Fairest of for_tune bless thy way— Light of my life, fare_well!

Rose of my fan-cy's gar-den fair, Fortune foretells Joy that ex-cels—

Al-mond-eyed maid of beau-ty rare, Fondest of fond fare-wells!...

MIMOSA.

Poco più vivo.

MIM.

So-rry and sad I go from thee, Lord of my lov-ing heart!

MIM.

Ever and ev-er think of me, Though for a time we part. Saved by a friend from

MIM.

hap-less fate, Whither she goes go I; So till I come, my sol-dier, wait!

MIM.

So till I come— good-bye!. So till I come— good-bye!

MIM.

Son of the sword, whose gleaming blade Guarding its prize Danger defies, Truest of knights to trusting maid,

MIM.

Sweetest of sweet good-byes! . . . .

Allegro vivo.

MOLLY.

Oh, what will they do with Mol - ly, With poor lit-tle mad-cap me? I've got in a mess In a Jap-an-ese dress, And what will the consequence be? No doubt with a girl like Mol-ly They'd try to take li-ber-ties free, But

M.

if they've the fol_ly To take them with Molly, They'll have to be sharper than shel

Now

Now

Now

Now

who is this Ro - li Po - li, And what is her lit - tle game? We're

who is this Ro - li Po - li, And what is her lit - tle game? We're

who is this Ro - li Po - li, And what is her lit - tle game? We're

who is this Ro - li Po - li, And what is her lit - tle game? We're bound to admit That we're puzzled a bit, For no_body knows her by name. It's

bound to admit That we're puzzled a bit, For no_body knows her by name. It's

bound to admit That we're puzzled a bit, For no_body knows her by name. It's

bound to admit That we're puzzled a bit, For no_body knows her by name. It's

hard up_on Ro - li Po - li To hint that she's o_pen to doubt, And

hard up_on Ro - li Po - li To hint that she's o_pen to doubt, And

hard up_on Ro - li Po - li To hint that she's o_pen to doubt, And

hard up_on Ro - li Po - li To hint that she's o_pen to doubt, And yet we're suspicious, And rather am_bitious Of finding a thing or two out. And

yet we're suspicious, And rather am_bitious Of finding a thing or two out. And

yet we're suspicious, And rather am_bitious Of finding a thing or two out. And

yet we're suspicious, And rather am_bitious Of finding a thing or two out. And

yet we're sus-picious, And rather ambitious Of find_ing a thing or two out.

yet we're sus-picious, And rather am_bitious Of find_ing a thing or two out.

yet we're sus-picious, And rather am_bitious Of find_ing a thing or two out.

yet we're sus-picious And rather am_bitious Of find_ing a thing or two out.

An—o—ther ri—val! Though I'm rid of one, It seems my work is on—ly yet half done! Most no—ble! we're heart—bro—ken, I may say, To take Mi—mo—sa

98

from you. Laugh a _ way! But don't make sure you've got the best of

me! Take care, my lord. In Eng _ lish hands is

she; So don't you dare To touch a hair Of the head of that dain_ty

gei_sha fair! If truth be told To a Mar_quis old, It's you, not the girl, Who's

CHORUS.

just been sold! It's on _ _ ly the way Of sai _ lors gay, Yet it

It's on _ _ ly the way Of sai _ lors gay, Yet it

It's on _ _ ly the way Of sai _ lors gay, Yet it

It's on _ _ ly the way Of sai _ lors gay, Yet it

seems un _ common _ ly rude to say That if truth be told To a

seems un _ common _ ly rude to say That if truth be told To a

seems un _ common _ ly rude to say That if truth be told To a

seems un _ common _ ly rude to say That if truth be told To a

IMARI.

Mar - quis old, It's *he,* not the girl, who's just been sold! This

Mar - quis old, It's *he,* not the girl, who's just been sold!

Mar - quis old, It's *he,* not the girl, who's just been sold!

Mar - quis old, It's *he,* not the girl, who's just been sold!

con - - - ver - - sa - tion we will not pro - long— It

may turn out that af - ter all you're wrong!. . .

CHORUS.

Please to go! Please to go! Fast the sun is set_ting,

Please to go! Please to go! Fast the sun is set_ting,

Please to go! Please to go! Fast the sun is set.ting,

Please to go! Please to go! Fast the sun is set_ting,

Due res_pect to cus_tom show; Or_ders you're for_get_ting.

Due res_pect to cus_tom show; Or_ders you're for_get_ting.

Due res_pect to cus_tom show; Or_ders you're for_get_ting.

Due res_pect to cus_tom show; Or_ders you're for_get_ting.

Please to go! Please to go! Seek the ci - ty's shel - ter;

Please to go! Please to go! Seek the ci - ty's shel - ter;

Please to go! Please to go! Seek . the ci - ty's shel - ter;

Please to go! Please to go! Seek the ci - ty's shel - ter;

Time is press - ing— Swift progress - ing, Hur - ry hel - ter - skel - ter, hel - ter -

Time is press - ing— Swift progress - ing, Hur - ry hel - ter - skel - ter, hel - ter -

Time is press - ing— Swift progress - ing, Hur - ry hel - ter - skel - ter, hel - ter -

Time is press - ing— Swift progress - ing, Hur - ry hel - ter - skel - ter, hel - ter -

skel-ter hel-ter skel-ter! . . . . Please to go!
-skel-ter, hel-ter-skel-ter! . . . . Please to go!
-skel-ter, hel-ter-skel-ter! . . . . Please to go!
-skel-ter, hel-ter-skel-ter! . . . . Please to go!
Please to go!— Fast the sun is set-ting, Due res-pect to
Please to go!— Fast the sun is set-ting, Due res-pect to
Please to go!— Fast the sun is set-ting, Due res-pect to
Please to go!— Fast the sun is set-ting, Due res-pect to

cus-tom show; Or-ders you're for- -get - ting. Please to go!

cus-tom show; Or-ders you're for-get-ting. Please to go!

cus-tom show; Or-ders you're for- -get - ting. Please to go!

cus-tom show; Or-ders you're for- -get - ting. Please to go!

Please to go! Seek the ci-ty's shel-ter; Time is pressing—

Please to go! Seek the ci-ty's shel-ter; Time is pressing—

Please to go! Seek the ci-ty's shel-ter; Time is pressing—

Please to go! Seek the ci-ty's shel-ter; Time is pressing—

Swift progress - ing, Hur - - ry hel ter - skel - ter, hel - ter -
Swift progress - ing, Hur - - ry hel - ter - skel - ter, hel - ter -
Swift progress - ing, Hur - - ry hel - ter - skel - ter, hel - ter -
Swift progress - ing, Hur - - ry hel - ter - skel - ter, hel - ter -
- skel - ter, hel - ter - skel - ter, hel - ter - skel - - - - - - - - -
- skel - ter, hel - ter - skel - ter, hel - ter - skel - - - - - - -
- skel - ter, hel - ter - skel - ter, hel - ter - skel - - - - - - - -
- skel - ter, hel - ter - skel - ter, hel - ter - skel - - - - - - - - -

106

- ter! . . . .

- ter! . . . .

- ter! . . . .

- ter! . . . .

loco.

END OF ACT 1.

No 15. ENTR'ACTE.

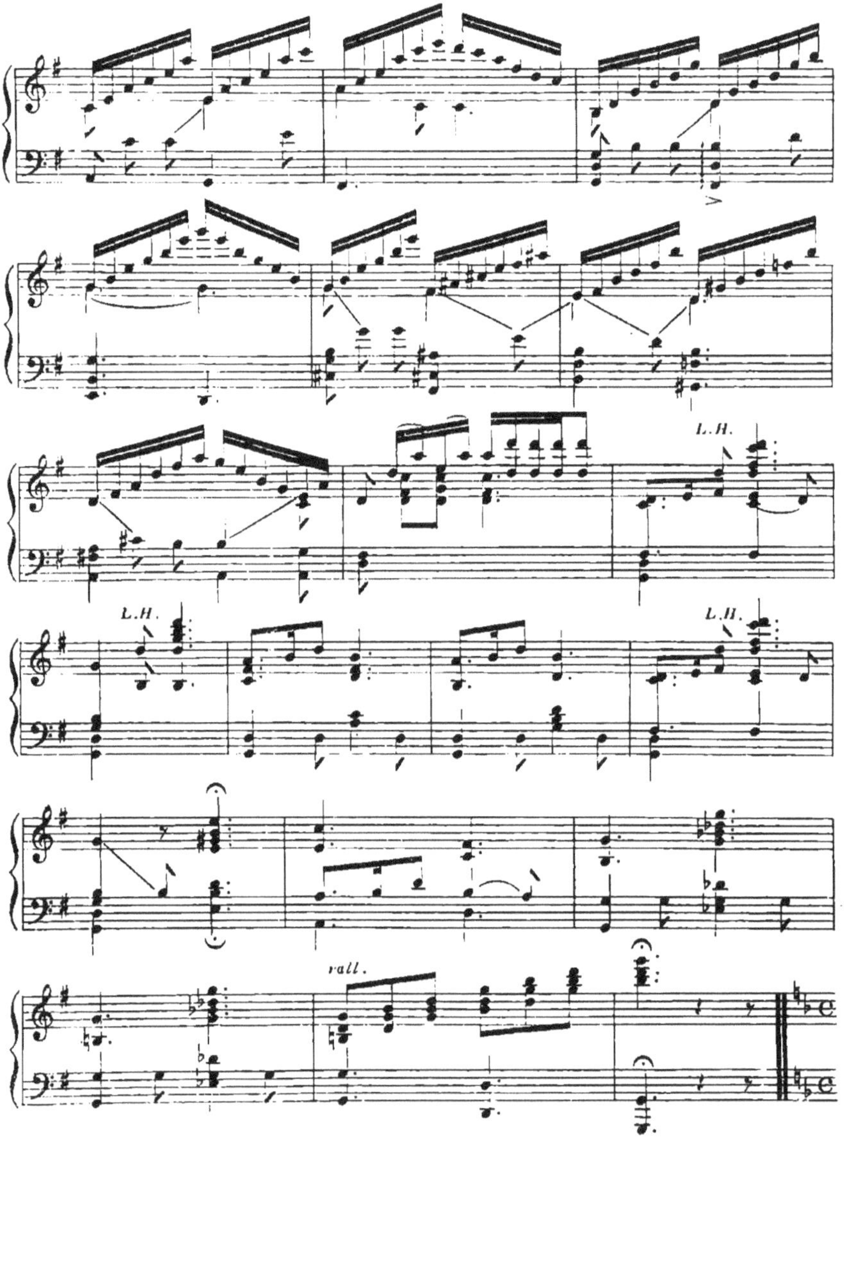
L.H.
L.H.
L.H.
rall.

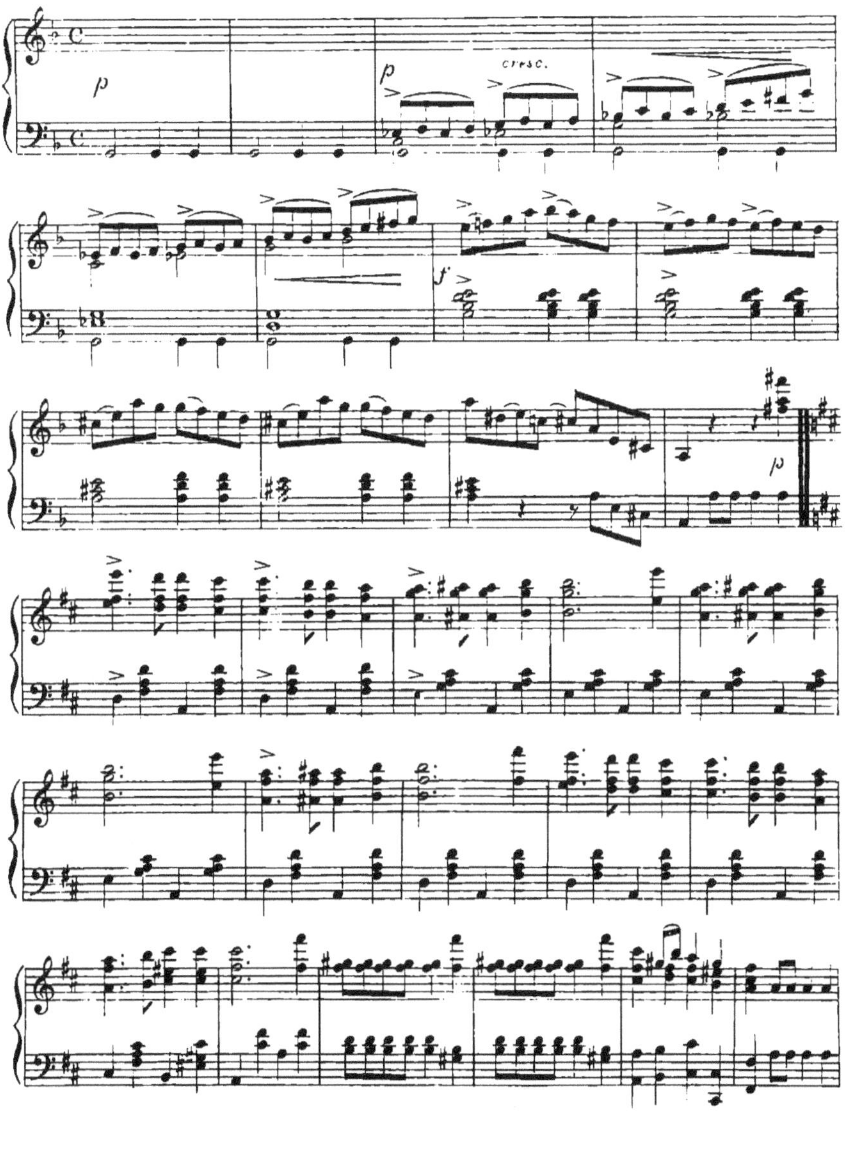
p
p
cresc.
f
p

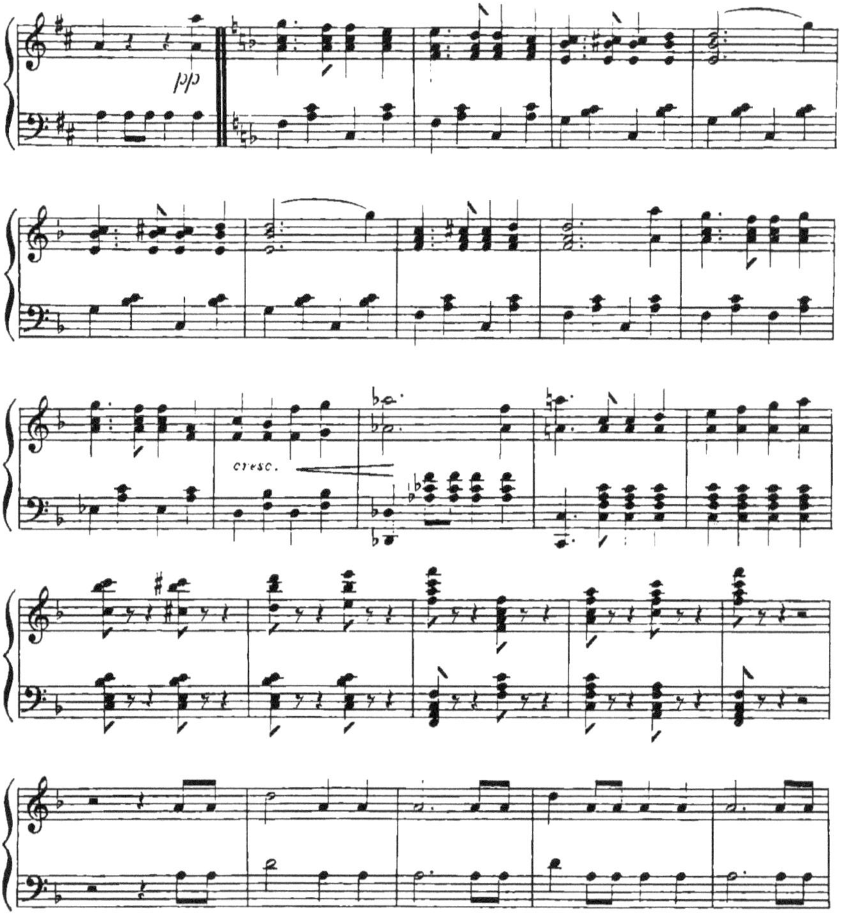
pp
cresc.

Nᵒ 16. OPENING CHORUS. ACT II.—"DAY BORN OF LOVE."

SOPRANO. / ALTO. / TENOR. / BASS. / PIANO.

Day born of love, Of gladness and de - light, Your

mo - ments soon in - vite To mys - tic mar - riage rite! ....

Thron'd high a _ bove, O Ten _ to Su ma shines, And laughing he di _

Thron'd high a _ bove, O Ten _ to Su ma shines, And laughing he di _

Thron'd high a _ bove, O Ten _ to Su ma shines, And laughing he di _

Thron'd high a _ bove, O Ten _ to Su ma shines, And laughing he di _

vines   A   lov _ er's   sweet de _ signs...............

_ vines   A   lov _ er's   sweet de _ signs...............

_ vines   A   lov _ er's   sweet de _ signs...............

_ vines   A   lov _ er's   sweet de _ signs...............

O - ha - yo! O - ha - yo! Moon by night and sun by day
O - ha - yo! O - ha - yo! Moon by night and sun by day
O - ha - yo! O - ha - yo! Moon by night and sun by day
O - ha - yo! O - ha - yo! Moon by night and sun by day
Ten - der beam and bla - zing ray! O - ha - yo!
Ten - der beam and bla - zing ray! O - ha - yo!
Ten - der beam and bla - zing ray! O - ha - yo!
Ten - der beam and bla - zing ray! O - ha - yo!

O _ ha _ yo! Watch and ward o'er lovers keep! Day to drink of pleasure deep,

O _ ha _ yo! Watch and ward o'er lovers keep! Day to drink of pleasure deep,

O _ ha _ yo! Watch and ward o'er lovers keep! Day to drink of pleasure deep,

O _ ha _ yo! Watch and ward o'er lovers keep! Day to drink of pleasure deep,

Night for rest and gen _ tle sleep Night for rest and sleep.

Night for rest and gen _ tle sleep Night for rest and sleep.

Night for rest and gen _ tle sleep Night for rest and sleep.

Night for rest and gen _ tle sleep Night for rest and sleep.

Day born of love, Of glad.ness and de _ light Your

Day born of love, Of glad.ness and de _ light Your

Day born of love, Of glad.ness and de _ light Your

Day born of love, Of glad.ness and de _ light Your

mo.ments soon in _ vite To mys _ tic mar.riage rite!

mo.ments soon in _ vite To mys _ tic mar.riage rite!

mo.ments soon in _ vite To mys _ tic mar.riage rite!

mo.ments soon in _ vite To mys _ tic mar.riage rite!

Po _ lite _ ly dress'd In all our best, The wed _ ding we a _

Po _ lite _ ly dress'd In all our best, The wed _ ding we a _

Po _ lite _ ly dress'd In all our best, The wed _ ding we a _

Po _ lite _ ly dress'd In all our best, The wed _ ding we a _

_ wait, And hope they wont be late, Or else for _ get the date. What

_ wait, And hope they wont be late, Or else for _ get the date. What

_ wait, And hope they wont be late, Or else for _ get the date. What

_ wait, And hope they wont be late, Or else for _ get the date. What would be done If ei _ ther one Neg _ lec _ ted to ap _ pear; If some-body demurr'd Or

would be done If ei _ ther one Neg _ lec _ ted to ap _ pear; If some-body demurr'd Or

would be done If ei _ ther one Neg _ lec _ ted to ap _ pear; If some-body demurr'd Or

would be done If ei _ ther one Neg _ lec _ ted to ap _ pear; If some-body demurr'd Or

a _ ny-thing occurr'd With all to in _ ter _ fere? Be _ fore our eyes The

a _ ny-thing occurr'd With all to in _ ter _ fere? Be _ fore our eyes The

a _ ny-thing occurr'd With all to in _ ter _ fere? Be _ fore our eyes The

a _ ny-thing occurr'd With all to in _ ter _ fere? Be _ fore our eyes The

118

prospect lies Of rich and fes_tive fare, With cups of sa _ ke' rare To

prospect lies Of rich and fes_tive fare, With cups of sa _ ke' rare To

prospect lies Of rich and fes_tive fare, With cups of sa _ ke' rare To

prospect lies Of rich and fes_tive fare, With cups of sa _ ke' rare To

toast the hap_py pair. No won_der then That maids and men U _ nite in Hy_men's

toast the hap_py pair. No won_der then That maids and men U _ nite in Hy_men's

toast the hap_py pair. No won_der then That maids and men U _ nite in Hy_men's

toast the hap_py pair. No won_der then That maids and men U _ nite in Hy_men's praise, And sing their joy _ ous lays With blushes all .... a -

praise, And sing their joy _ ous lays With blushes all .... a -

praise, And sing their joy _ ous lays With blushes all .... a -

praise, And sing their joy _ ous lays With blushes all .... a -

_ blaze!...............

_ blaze!...............

_ blaze!...............

_ blaze!...............

Nº 17. SONG—(MOLLY.) "THE TOY MONKEY."

COMPOSED BY LIONEL MONCKTON.

1. Poor lit-tle maid-en, who loves a bit of fun, Learns her pro-pen-si-ty to rue!
2. No-to-dy doubts that this hor-rid Ja-pan-ese Wives-o-ri-en-tal-ly-has got;

M.

Just look at me! what a pret _ ty thing I've done!
One, two or three, or as ma _ ny as you please—

M.

Here's a de _ light _ ful how - de - do! A pre _ cious pic _ kle I'm in!
I won't be ad _ ded to the lot! He thinks I can't re _ sist him;

M.

Fool _ ish lit _ tle Mol _ ly, Punish'd for your fol _ ly, A wood _ en
Roll _ ing in his rich _ es, Fan _ cies he be _ witch _ es— B _ t round my

M.

mon _ key climb _ in' Is _ n't on a stick like you!
thumb I'll twist him Whe _ ther he's a _ ware or no! !

poco rit:

CHORUS.

Click! click! I'm a mon-key on a stick! A - ny one with me can
Click! click! He's a mon-key on a stick, Bound to let me have my

play, And my an - tics he'll en-joy Till he finds a new-er toy.When he'll
way! So I'll keep him all a-live Till my English friends arrive-When I'll

1º
wish me a po-lite good - day......
wish him a po-lite good -

2º
- day! .....

cresc.

D.C.

DANCE (After 2nd verse.)

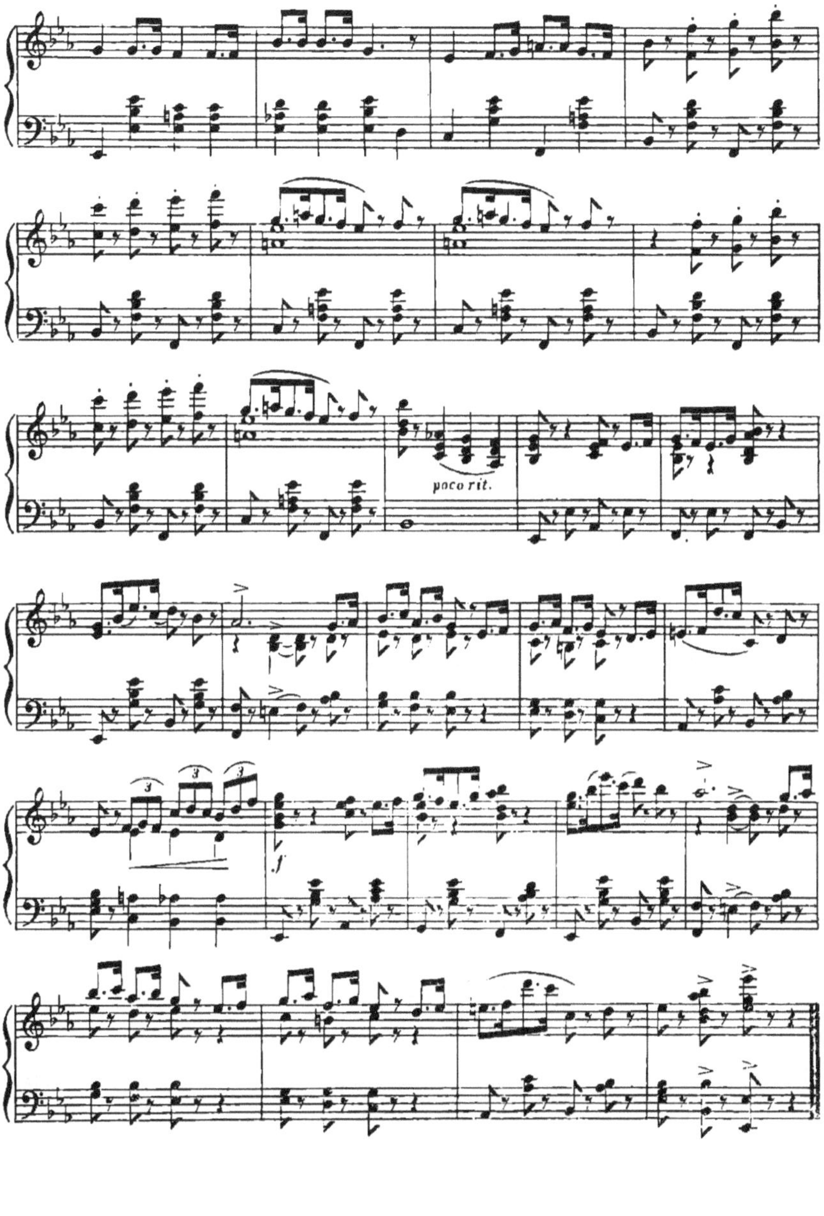
poco rit.
f

124

Nº 18. DUET — (JULIETTE & WUN-HI.) "CHING-A-RING-A-REE!"

Allegretto.

PIANO.

JULI. When *I* want a _ _ _ ny _ _ thing done, I
WUN-HI. When *me* want get _ _ too my way, Keep

try my fa _ vour _ ite plan — I whee _ dle and coax, And
much _ ee o _ _ _ _ pen eyes; For Chi _ na _ man mild Him

Copyright **1896**, by Hopwood & Crew.

flat - ter the folks As on - ly a French girl can! If
well - ee sharp child - Tell plen - ty big whop - - per lies! JULI. To -
e - ver I chance on one Who won't be coax'd by
- ge - ther we'll work to - day - You're just the man for
me, I peep and I pry, And I work on the sly - Com -
me! A girl ne - ver jibs At a few lit - tle fibs - Com -
WUN-HI.
JULIETTE.
WUN-HI.
- pren - ez - vous ca? Wee! Wee! Com - - - pren - ez - vous ca? Wee!
- pren - ez - vous ca? Wee! Wee! Com - - - pren - ez - vous ca? Wee!

126

cute Chi _ nee! Mon _ sieur, mam'selle Suit ve_ry ve_ry well. So sing Ching-a-ring Ching-a-

ring - a - ring - a - ree! DANCE *(after second verse.)*

mf

D.C.

f

No. 19. CONCERTED PIECE—"GEISHA ARE WE."

Gei-sha are we, Bid-den to be Present to-day at the ce-re-mo-nee;

Each in her best, Dain-ti-ly dress'd Brings en-ter-tainment for ev-e-ry guest.

4 G.
Smart lit-tle maid, Versed in her trade, Knows what will please when ex-pressive-ly play'd,
4 G.
Guess-es what dance All will en-trance, Aid-ed by sau-cy and mis-chie-vous glance.
4 G.
Gei-sha are we, Bidden to be Present to-day at the ce-re-mo-nee;
4 G.
Each in her best, Dain-ti-ly dress'd Brings entertainment for ev-e-ry guest.

130

OFFICERS.

Now, be_ _fore we let you go, Tell us

ev'_ ry_thing you know, For our spirits ra_ther low your words may hap_pen ease. Will the

wedding be a treat? Are there lots of things to eat? Is the bride extremely sweet and very

4 GEISHA.

Jap_an_ese? Is the bride extremely sweet and very Japan_ese? Oh you

131

mus_n't ask us ques_tions and de_tain us all the day, For you're

naugh_ty Eng_lish sai_lors, and we don't know what you'll say! Yes, the

bride is ve_ry charm_ing, but it is_n't your af_fair, So you'll

please to let us go, and oh! we won_der how you dare! If the

CUNNINGHAM.

C.
Mar - quis should de - tect This flir - - ta - tion in - cor - rect, His au -
C.
- tho - ri - ty un - check'd He will as - - sert with us. But you're
C.
all so ve - ry nice That with - - out re - flect - ing twice, We in - -
C.
- tend to break the ice, And make you flirt with us.

ENGLISH GIRLS.
Now you mustn't go and leave us for the geisha, if you please, For we
ff
E.G.
cannot have you flirt_ing with these pretty Jap_an_ese! They are charming lit_tle creatures, but it
E.G.
4 GEISHA.
real_ly is_n't fair, So you'll please to let them go, and oh! we won_der how you dare! Yes we
4 G.
OFFICERS.
won_der how they dare! Yes we wonder how we dare!

134

GEISHA.

Gei - sha are we, Bid - den to be Pre - sent to - day at the
ce - re - mo - nee; Each in her best Dain - ti - ly dress'd
Brings en - ter - tain - ment for ev - e - ry guest. Brings en - ter - tain - ment for
ev - e - ry guest.

dim:

ppp

No 20. SONG — (FAIRFAX.) "STAR OF MY SOUL."

1. How can I wait— when she I worship on_ly,
2. Glo_ry of flow'rs and fai_ry-land a_round me,

Friend_less and fair, my help may sore_ly need? How can I wait, and
O_ver my path the joy_ous sunlight falls; Yet is my dear, whose

leave her sad and lone_ly, Count_ing the hours that all too slow_ly speed?
charms so fast have bound me, Caged like a bird with-in those gild_ed walls.

Earth has no grace that does not cling a_bout her— Life has no charm, if mine she
Would I could break the cru_el bonds that hold her, Snap ev_'ry chain that keeps us

may not be; Star of my soul! I can_not live with_out her;
two a_part! Star of my soul!— the half I have not told her

O grant this day may give her back to me!
Of all the love that fills my beat_ing heart!

rall: pp

Dream, O my dear-est, till we meet once more, Day-dreams of hap-pi-ness a-
-gain in store, Dreams of a fu-ture that our fates may hold,
1st time.
Pass'd in the wonder-land of love un-told!
mf
D.C.
2nd time.
Pass'd in the won-der-land of love un-told!

N.º 21. SONG— (JULIETTE.) "IF THAT'S NOT LOVE— WHAT IS?"

Allegro moderato.

PIANO.

Fine

J.

1. To win the man who's won my heart There's no _ thing that I
2. To win his heart— if he were rich— Still fur _ ther I'd con _

J.

would _ n't do! I'd wear a frock that was _ n't smart— An un _ _ be _ com _ ing
_ sent to go! I'd catch his eye by con _ duct which Would not be vo _ ted

J.

cha _ peau too. If square-cut shoes should please his taste, Then no more point _ ed
comme il faut. I'd prove to him in tête - à - tête That girls are not so

J.
toes for me, And thir - ty in - ches round the waist I'd cheer - ful - ly.. con -
prim and chill, And then if he should he - - si - tate-- I'd go a lit - - tle
- sent to be. And if *that's* not love - what
fur - ther still! And if *that's* not love - what
is? For I feel my heart go pop, And my sen - ses whirl and
is? For I feel my heart go pop, And my sen - ses whirl and
fizz Till I don't know where to stop!
fizz Till I don't know where to stop!
f
p

Car c'est ain_si, mes a_mis,..... Que l'on aime en tous pays

... Car l'a_mour, l'a_mour, l'a_mour, l'a_mour, L'a_mour ne rai_son_ne

pas!...... Car l'a_mour, l'a_mour, l'a_mour, l'a_mour, L'a

mour ne raison_ne pas! mour ne raison_ne pas!....

D.C. to Sym. D.C. to Sym.

No 21. JAPANESE MARCH. (ENTRANCE OF CHORUS.)

Ko _ i _ wa se_ni sumu, Tori _ wa ki_ni tomaru, Hi_to_wa nasake _ no

Ko _ i _ wa se_ni sumu, Tori _ wa ki_ni tomaru, Hi_to_wa nasake _ no

Ko _ i _ wa se_ni sumu, Tori _ wa ki_ni tomaru, Hi_to_wa nasake _ no

Ko _ i _ wa se_ni sumu, Tori _ wa ki_ni tomaru, Hi_to_wa nasake _ no

Ka_ge........... Ko_i _ wa se_ni sumu, Tor_i _ wa ki_ni tomaru, Hi _ to_wa
Ka_ge........... Ko_i _ wa se_ni sumu, Tor_i _ wa ki_ni tomaru, Hi _ to_wa
Ka_ge........... Ko_i _ wa se_ni sumu, Tor_i _ wa ki_ni tomaru, Hi _ to_wa
Ka_ge........... Ko_i _ wa se_ni sumu, Tor_i _ wa ki_ni tomaru, Hi _ to_wa
na_sa_ke_no Ka_ge, Ka_ge, Ka_ge, Ka_ge _ ni.
na_sa_ke_no Ka_ge, Ka_ge, Ka_ge, Ka_ge _ ni.
na_sa_ke_no Ka_ge, Ka_ge, Ka_ge, Ka_ge _ ni.
na_sa_ke_no Ka_ge, Ka_ge, Ka_ge, Ka_ge _ ni.

No. 23. ENTRANCE OF GEISHA—"WITH SPLENDOUR AUSPICIOUS."

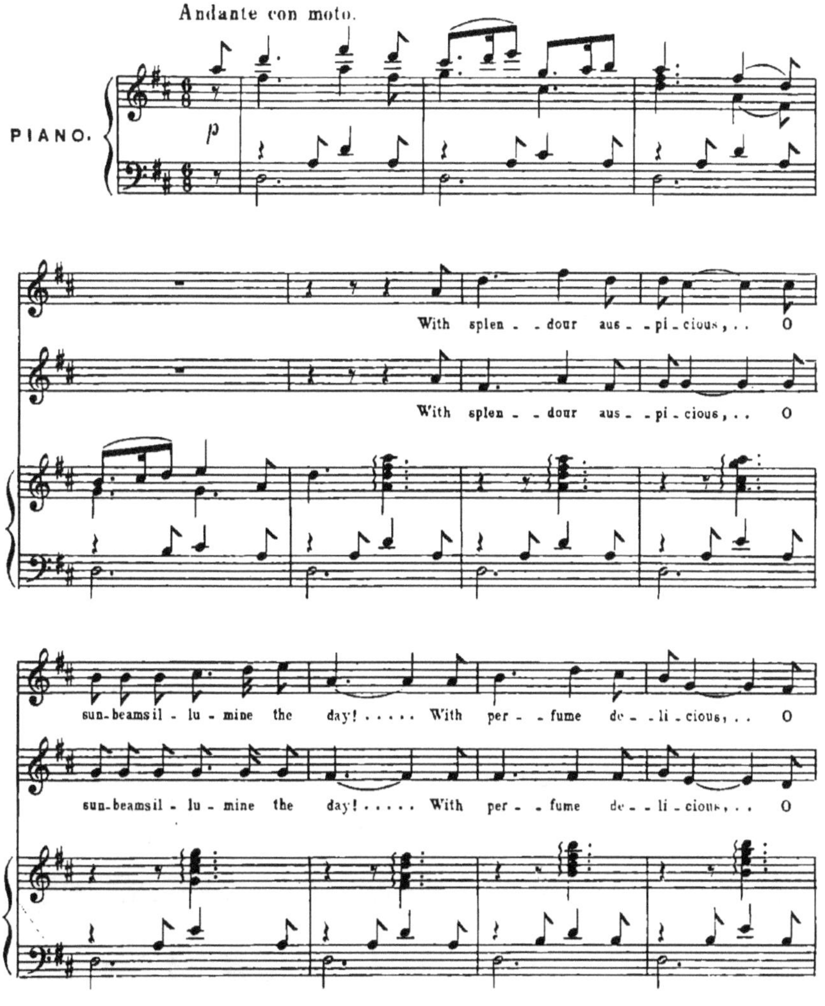

flowers make fragrant the way!..... O ze - phyrs, go car-ry..... Our

flowers make fragrant the way!..... O ze - phyrs, go car-ry..... Our

song to the Mas - ter of Might,..... Who com - - - eth to

song to the Mas - ter of Might,..... Who com - - - eth to

mar - ry...... The Rose of his fan - cy's de - - light!...... Sing

mar - ry...... The Rose of his fan - cy's de - - light!...... Sing

sweet - ly and shril - ly, ... O twit - ter - ing birds of the
sweet - ly and shril - ly, ... O twit - ter - ing birds of the
air! . . . . Than li - lac or li - ly. . . . . The bride is more dain - ti - ly
air! . . . . Than li - lac or li - ly. . . . . The bride is more dain - ti - ly
fair . . . . From hill and from val - ley . . . . . The
fair . . . . From hill and from val - ley . . . . . The

e-choes are greet-ing the day . . . . . With soft fal - lal-lal-ly, . . . And
e-choes are greet-ing the day . . . . . With soft fal - lal-lal-ly, . . . And
Meno mosso.
ten-der fal-lal-lal-lal - lay! . . . . And ten-der fal-lal-lal-lal - lay! . . . . And
ten-der fal-lal-lal-lal - lay! . . . . And ten-der fal-lal-lal-lal - lay! . . . . And
a tempo.
ten - der fal - lal - lal - lal - lay! Ah! . . . . With
ten - der fal - lal - lal - lal - lay! Ah! . . . . With
a tempo.

splen - - dour aus - pi - cious, .. O sun-beams il - lu - mine the day! . . . . With

splen - - dour aus - pi - cious, .. O sun-beams il - lu - mine the day! . . . . With

pp

per - - - fume de - li - cious, .. O flow-ers make fragrant the way! . . . . . O

per - - fume de - li - cious, .. O flow-ers make fragrant the way! . . . . . O

ze - - - phyrs, go car - ry . . . . Our song to the Mas-ter of Might, ... Who

ze - - - phyrs, go car - ry . . . . Our song to the Mas-ter of Might, ... Who

com - - eth to mar - ry . . . . . The Rose of his fancy's de - light, . . . The
com - - eth to mar - ry . . . . . The Rose of his fancy's de - light, ... The
Rose of his fancy's de - - light, ... The Rose of his fancy's de - light! . . . .
Rose of his fancy's de - - light, ... The Rose of his fancy's de - light! . . . .
8va

Nº 24. SONG — (WUN-HI & CHORUS.) "CHIN CHIN CHINAMAN."

1. Chi-na-man no mo-ney ma-kee   Al-lo li-fee long!   Washee-washee once me ta-kee—
2. When me get-tee catchee cheatee   Play-ing pie-cee card,   Chi-na-man they al-lo beat-ee—

Washee-washee wrong!   When me thinkee steal-ee col-lars   P'licee-man-ee come;
Kickee wellee hard!   When me ta-kee ni-cee pla-cee   Ma-kee plen-ty tea,

W.-H.

Me get fi_nee fi_vee dol_lars— Plen_ty muchee sum!
Get_tee me in more dis_gra_cee— Up they sell_ee me!

W.-H.

Chin chin Chi_na_man Muchee muchee sad! Me a_fraid Al_lo trade
Chin chin Chi_na_man Muchee muchee sad! Me a_fraid Al_lo trade

W.-H.

Well_ee well_ee sad! No_ee joke— Bro_kee broke— Ma_kee shut_tee shop!
Well_ee well_ee sad! No_ee joke— Bro_kee broke— Ma_kee shut_tee shop!

W.-H.

Chin chin Chi_na_man, Chop, chop, chop!
Chin chin Chi_na_man, Chop, chop, chop!

CHORUS.

Chin chin Chi na man Much ee much ee sad!

Chin chin Chi na man Much ee much ee sad!

Chin chin Chi na man Much ee much ee sad!

Chin chin Chi na man Much ee much ee sad!

He a fraid Al lo trade Well ee well ee bad!

He a fraid Al lo trade Well ee well ee bad!

He a fraid Al lo trade Well ee well ee bad!

He a fraid Al lo trade Well ee well ee bad!

DANCE.

PIANO

Più mosso.

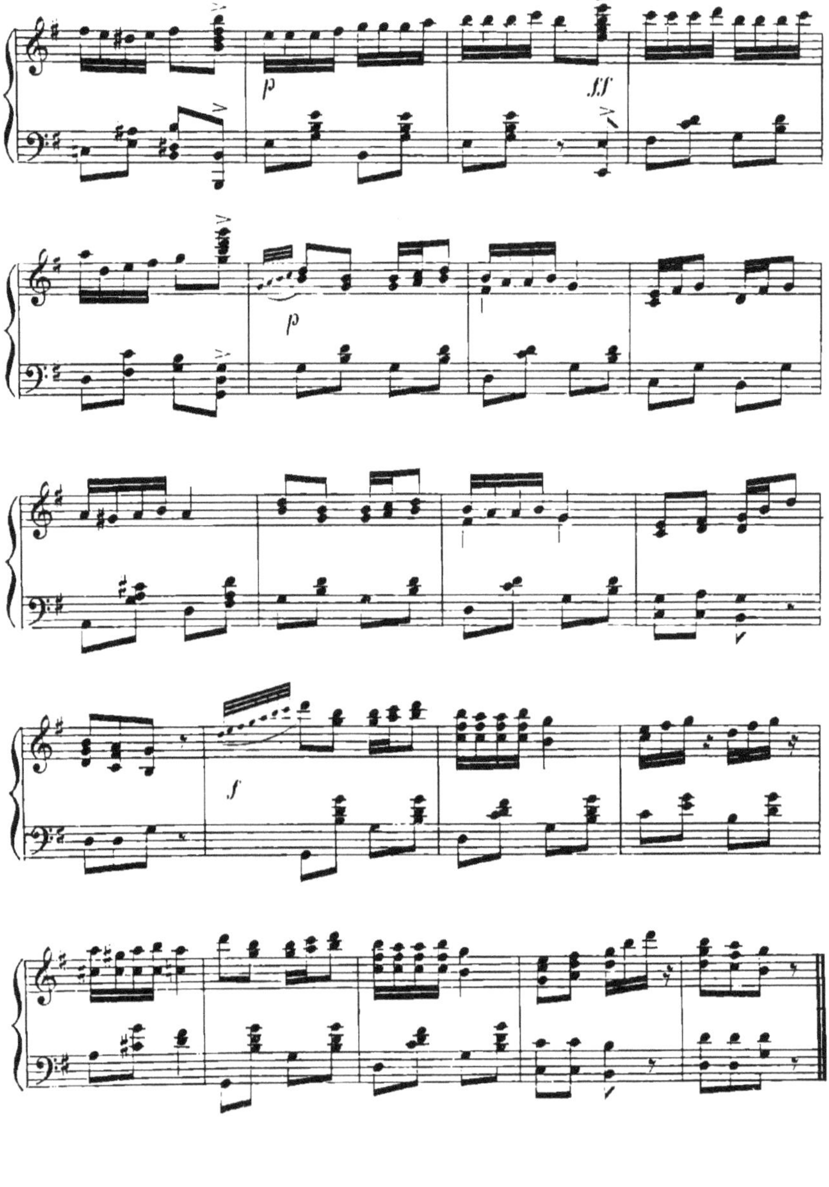
p
ff
p
f

No. 25. SONG.—(FAIRFAX & CHORUS.) LOVE! LOVE!

Oh,
When

lit - tle laugh-ing god of Love, In kind - ly mood you seem to be, Though
lov - ers woo in ac-cents soft, You laugh at hopes that prom - ise fair, And

sea - ted on your perch a-bove You smile at lov - ers' mis - er - y! For
still you sit and laugh a - loft When love is hate and hope des pair! As

man to you is but a toy, And yet you some - times deign to hear; To-
clay with - in your hands are we, And yet you've cas'd my... heart's a - larms, For

day you fill my heart with joy_ To - day you give me back my dear!
she who's all the world to me Will soon be safe with - in my arms!
Tempo di Valse.
più lento
Ah!......................
Love! love! soft-ly you
p
pp
poco più mosso
call; Love! love! laughing at all! Mis-chiev-ous Cu-pid with
rall.
am - or - ous dart, Man's at your mer-cy for you rule his heart!
rall.

a tempo di valse.

Love! love! soft-ly you call; Love! love! laughing at all!

Love! love! soft-ly you call; Love! love! laughing at all!

Love! love! soft-ly you call; Love! love! laughing at all!

Love! love! soft-ly you call; Love! love! laughing at all!

Love! love! soft-ly you call; Love! love! laughing at all!

Mis-chiev-ous Cu-pid with am-or-ous dart, Man's at your mer-cy for you rule his heart!

Mis-chiev-ous Cu-pid with am-or-ous dart,..........

Mis-chiev-ous Cu-pid with am-or-ous dart,..........

Mis-chiev-ous Cu-pid with am-or-ous dart,..........

Mis-chiev-ous Cu-pid with am-or-ous dart,..........

2.
dim.
pp
mer - cy for you rule, for you rule his
Man's at your mer - cy for you rule his
heart!
dim.
ppp

Nᵒ 26. SONG—"HEY-DIDDLE-DIDDLE: WHEN MAN IS IN LOVE."

VOICE.

PIANO.

CUNNINGHAM.

He's long-ing to mar-ry a dear lit-tle bride, So beau-ti-ful, charming and
So come where the ban-quet is lav-ish-ly laid—Our wel-come is sure to be

sup-ple That peo-ple will say, as he walks at her side, "By
hear-ty; We'll learn from the lips of some quaint lit-tle maid The

CUN.
Jove! what a good look - ing cou - ple!"..... But won't he be wild when he
joys of a Ja - pan - ese par - ty!....... For dash - ing young sai - lors there's
CUN.
knows that we dare To laugh at his am - or - ous fol - ly, Be -
al - ways a charm In flirt - ing with short or with tall ones; I
CUN.
- cause we in - tend to take jol - ly good care He does - n't get mar - ried to
know I can do with a girl on each arm, And two on my knees if they're
CUN.
Mol - ly!
small ones!

CUN. For hey - did - dle - did - dle! when man is in love He
For hey - did - dle - did - dle! when man is in love He

CUN. thinks that he's luck-y all o-thers a-bove To wed such a squeez-a-ble,
thinks that he's luck-y all o-thers a-bove To wed an em-brace-a-ble,

CUN. Sit - on - your - knees - a - ble, Dear lit - tle du - ti - ful
Pat - on the - face - a - ble, Dear lit - tle du - ti - ful

CUN. duck of a dove, such a dear lit - tle duck of a dove!........
duck of a dove, such a dear lit - tle duck of a dove!........

162

CHORUS.

Yes, hey did - dle did - dle! when man is in love He
Yes, hey did - dle did - dle! when man is in love He

Yes, hey did - dle did - dle! when man is in love He
Yes, hey did - dle did - dle! when man is in love He

Yes, hey did dle did - dle! **when** man **is** in love He
Yes, hey - did dle did dle! **when** man **is** in love He

Yes, hey did - dle - did - dle! when man is in love He
Yes, hey - did - dle - did - dle! when man is in love He

thinks that he's luck - y all o - thers a - bove To
thinks that he's luck - y all o - thers a - bove To

thinks that he's luck - y all o - thers a - bove To
thinks that he's luck - y all o - thers a - bove To

thinks that he's luck y all o thers a bove To
thinks that he's luck - y all o thers a bove To

thinks that he's luck - y all o thers a bove To
thinks that he's luck - y all o thers a bove To

wed such a squeez - a - ble, Sit - on - your knees - a - ble,
wed an em - brace - a - ble, Pat - on - the face - a - ble,

wed such a squeez - a - ble, Sit - on - your knees - a - ble,
wed an em - brace - a - ble, Pat - on - the face - a - ble,

wed such a squeez - a - ble, Sit - on - your knees - a - ble,
wed an em - brace - a - ble, Pat - on - the face - a - ble,

wed such a squeez - a - ble, Sit - on - your knees - a - ble,
wed an em - brace - a - ble, Pat - on - the face - a - ble,

Dear lit - tle du - ti - ful duck of a dove, such a
Dear lit - tle du - ti - ful duck of a dove, such a

Dear lit - tle du - ti - ful duck of a dove, such a
Dear lit - tle du - ti - ful duck of a dove, such a

Dear lit - tle du - ti - ful duck of a dove, such a
Dear lit - tle du - ti - ful duck of a dove, such a

Dear lit - tle du - ti - ful duck of a dove, such a
Dear lit - tle du - ti - ful duck of a dove, such a

dear lit tle duck of a dove! ....
dear lit - tle duck of a dove! ....
dear lit - tle duck of a dove! ....
dear lit - tle duck of a dove! ....
dear lit - tle duck of a dove! ....
dear lit - tle duck of a dove! ....
dear lit - tle duck of a dove! ....
dear lit - tle duck of a dove! ....
DANCE.

Nº 27. SONG.— (MOLLY & CHORUS.) "THE INTERFERING PARROT."

Moderato.

PIANO.

MOLLY.

A par-rot once re-si-ded in a pret-ty gild-ed cage, Sar-
He left the poor ca-na-ry with her spi-rits ra-ther low, But
Ca-na-ry's yel-low coun-ten-ance with jea-lous-y wasgreen, And
Of course there is a mo-ral, and of course it's at the end— Those

_cas-tic was his tem-per, and un-cer-tain was his age, He
when she got her hus-band home her tongue be-gan to go. In
when he met his wife they had a nice do-mes-tic scene— Till-
fool-ish young ca-na-ries had a mon-key for a friend, And

knew that two canaries had a-partments overhead Who'd on-ly ve-ry re-cent-ly been
vain he tried cares-ses, and at-tempted to deny— The sil-ly lit-tle bird be-gan to
she with pocket handkerchief and he with sul-len scowl, They hurried off to Mª___ Jus-tice
as to all the trouble each in turn was giving vent, They put the cunning monkey on the

166

CHORUS.
1st & 2nd SOPRANOS.   MOLLY.

wed! They'd re_cent_ly been wed!   He   kept an eye on all that they were
cry! The bird be_gan to   cry!   She   told him that she knew he lov'd a_
Owl! To M!__ Jus_tice Owl!   He   grant_ed a ju_di_cial se _ par_
scent! They put him on the scent!   He   called up_on the par_rot in the

TEN.
They'd re_cent_ly been wed!
The bird be_gan to   cry!
To M!__ Jus_tice Owl!
They put him on the   scent!

BASS.
They'd re_cent_ly been wed!
The bird be_gan to   cry!
To M!__ Jus_tice Owl!
They put him on the   scent!

CHORUS.   MOLLY.

do _ ing—   An   in_ter_fer_ing parrot in a   nas_ty frame of mind! And
no _ ther—   A   shocking ac_cu_sa_tion for a lit_tle bird to make! And
_ a _ tion— And all because of Polly's un_sub_stan_ti_at_ed words! And
morn_ing—   No   doubt the par_rot wonder'd what on earth he had to say! And

An   in_ter_fer_ing parrot in a   nas_ty state of mind!
A   shocking ac_cu_sa_tion for a lit_tle bird to make!
And all because of Polly's un_sub_stan_ti_at_ed words!
No   doubt the par_rot wonder'd what on earth he had to say!

An   in_ter_fer_ing parrot in a   nas_ty state of mind!
A   shocking ac_cu_sa_tion for a lit_tle bird to make!
And all because of Polly's un_sub_stan_ti_at_ed words!
No   doubt the par_rot wonder'd what on earth he had to say!

M

vow'd he'd stop their bill _ ing and their coo _ ing.
said she meant to go and see her mo _ ther.
now they live in i _ cy i _ so _ la _ tion.
"went for" him with _ out the slight _ est warn _ ing.

Which
A
Two
The

Which
A
Two
The

Which
A
Two
The

real _ ly was ex _ ceed _ ing _ ly un _ kind! Ex _ ceed _ ing _ ly un _ kind!
ve _ ry sil _ ly step for her to take! A sil _ ly step to take!
real _ ly ve _ ry wretched lit _ tle birds! Two wretched lit _ tle birds!
par _ rot had a ve _ ry hap _ py day! A ve _ ry hap _ py day!

real _ ly was ex _ ceed _ ing _ ly un _ kind! Ex _ ceed _ ing _ ly un _ kind!
ve _ ry sil _ ly step for her to take! A sil _ ly step to take!
real _ ly ve _ ry wretched lit _ tle birds! Two wretched lit _ tle birds!
par _ rot had a ve _ ry hap _ py day! A ve _ ry hap _ py day!

real _ ly was ex _ ceed _ ing _ ly un _ kind! Ex _ ceed _ ing _ ly un _ kind!
ve _ ry sil _ ly step for her to take! A sil _ ly step to take!
real _ ly ve _ ry wretched lit _ tle birds! Two wretched lit _ tle birds!
par _ rot had a ve _ ry hap _ py day! A ve _ ry hap _ py day!

MOLLY.

Pol-ly winked his eye, and Pol-ly gave a sigh, And
Pol-ly winked his eye, and Pol-ly gave a sigh, And
Pol-ly winked his eye, and Pol-ly gave a sigh, And
Pol-ly piped his eye, and Pol-ly gave a sigh, And

ppp

Pol-ly took his best hat down; He
Pol-ly took his best hat down; He
Pol-ly bought a Spe-cial Sun. He
Pol-ly used a naugh-ty word. The

called on Mrs. C. and took a cup of tea. When
knew there'd be a fuss, so jump-ing on a 'bus, He
read the full re-port of what oc-curr'd in Court, And
mon-key-when he'd done— of fea-thers hard-ly one Had

Mr. C. had gone to town; Then wise-ly wagg'd his
called on Mr. C. in town; Then wise-ly wagg'd his
chuc-kled at the mis-chief done; Then go-ing off to
left up-on the bad old bird, He scratch'd his ach-ing

head, And se_ri_ous_ly said:— "Well, hus_bands are a
head And se_ri_ous ly said:— "A pret_ty wife you've
bed, Con_tent_ed_ly he said:— "Thank good_ness that's all
head, And rue_ful_ly he said:— "Oh, Sa_rah, ain't it

lot! A pret_ty one you've got! Such tales I ne_ver
got! I see you've had it hot, And bless your heart, it's
right! I'll get some sleep to - night— A thing I can_not
prime? I've had a beast_ly time! Poor Pol_ly's feel_ing

heard! So dis_so_lute a bird I ne_ver met be_
true She's just as bad as you! Di_rect_ly you are
do When lo_vers bill and coo, They won't an_noy a
bad— Oh, what a day I've had! I'm sor_ry on the

_fore! What go_ings on! Oh, lor!"
gone— Oh, don't she car_ry on!"
soul! Poor Pol_ly! scratch a poll!"
whole— Poor Pol_ly! scratch a poll!"

CHORUS.

Pol-ly winked his eye, and Pol-ly gave a sigh. And
Pol-ly winked his eye, and Pol-ly gave a sigh, And
Pol-ly winked his eye, and Pol-ly gave a sigh. And
Pol-ly piped his eye, and Pol-ly gave a sigh, And

Pol-ly winked his eye, and Pol-ly gave a sigh, And
Pol-ly winked his eye, and Pol-ly gave a sigh, And
Pol-ly winked his eye. and Pol-ly gave a sigh, And
Pol-ly piped his eye, and Pol-ly gave a sigh, And

Pol-ly winked his eye, and Pol-ly gave a sigh, And
Pol-ly winked his eye, and Pol-ly gave a sigh, And
Pol-ly winked his eye. and Pol-ly gave a sigh, And
Pol-ly piped his eye, and Pol-ly gave a sigh, And

Pol-ly took his best hat down; He
Pol-ly took his best hat down; He
Pol-ly bought a Spe-cial Sun. He
Pol-ly used a naugh-ty word. The

Pol-ly took his best hat down; He
Pol-ly took his best hat down; He
Pol-ly bought a Spe-cial Sun. He
Pol-ly used a naugh-ty word. The

Pol-ly took his best hat down; He
Pol-ly took his best hat down; He
Pol-ly bought a Spe-cial Sun. He
Pol-ly used a naugh-ty word. The

called on Mrs. — C. and took a cup of tea When
knew there'd be a fuss, so jumping on a 'bus, He
read the full re - port of what oc - curr'd in Court, And
mon - key when he'd done of fea - thers hard - ly one Had
called on Mrs. — C. and took a cup of tea When
knew there'd be a fuss, so jump - ing in a 'bus, He
read the full re - port of what oc - curr'd in Court, And
mon - key when he'd done of fea - thers hard - ly one Had
called on Mrs. — C. and took a cup of tea When
knew there'd be a fuss, so jump - ing in a 'bus, He
read the full re - port of what oc - curr'd in Court, And
mon - key when he'd done of fea - thers hard - ly one Had
1º 2º 3º
Last.
Mr. — C. had gone to town.
called on Mr. — C. in town.
chuckled at the mis - chief done.
left up - on the bad old bird.
Mr. C. had gone to town.
called on Mr. — C. in town.
chuckled at the mis - chief done.
left up - on the bad old bird.
Mr. C. had gone to town.
called on Mr. — C. in town.
chuckled at the mis - chief done.
left up - on the bad old bird.
p
ff
D.C.

Nᵒ 28. FINALE.— "BEFORE OUR EYES."

SOPRANO.

Be _ fore our eyes The pros _ pect lies Of

ALTO.

Be _ fore our eyes The pros _ pect lies Of

TENOR.

Be _ fore our eyes The pros _ pect lies Of

BASS.

Be _ fore our eyes The pros _ pect lies Of

PIANO.

rich and fes _ tive fare, With cups of sa _ ke' rare To toast the hap _ py

rich and fes _ tive fare, With cups of sa _ ke' rare To toast the hap _ py

rich and fes _ tive fare, With cups of sa _ ke' rare To toast the hap _ py

rich and fes _ tive fare, With cups of sa _ ke' rare To toast the hap _ py

pair. No won-der then That maids and men U - nite in Hy-men's praise, And
pair. No won-der then That maids and men U - nite in Hy-men's praise, And
pair. No won-der then That maids and men U - nite in Hy-men's praise, And
pair. No won-der then That maids and men U - nite in Hy-men's praise, And
Tempo di Valse.
sing their joy - ous lays, their joy - ous lays!....................
sing their joy - ous lays, their, joy - ous lays!....................
sing their joy - ous lays, their, joy - ous lays!....................
sing their joy - ous lays, their joy - ous lays!....................
Tempo di Valse.

174

Happy Japan, Garden of glitter! Flower and fan

Flutter and flitter; Land of bamboo, (Juvenile whacker!)

Por-ce-lain too, Tea-tray and lac-quer! Hap-py Ja-pan,
Por-ce-lain too, Tea-tray and lac-quer! Hap-py Ja-pan,
Por-ce-lain too, Tea-tray and lac-quer! Hap-py Ja-pan,
Por-ce-lain too, Tea-tray and lac-quer! Hap-py Ja-pan,
Hap-py Ja-pan, Hap-py Ja-pan!
Hap-py Ja-pan, Hap-py Ja-pan!
Hap-py Ja-pan, Hap-py Ja-pan!
Hap-py Ja-pan, Hap-py Ja-pan!
ff
8va

Nº 29. QUARTETTE — "WHAT WILL THE MARQUIS DO?"

(MIMOSA, FAIRFAX, CUNNINGHAM & WUN-HI.)

PIANO. *mf*

(FAIRFAX.) When he finds that his dear lit-tle love-bird's gone, Oh,
(MIMOSA.) When he finds that his dear lit-tle bride has fled, Oh,

what will the Mar-quis do?— Will he fly in-to a rage, Or
what will the Mar-quis do?— If he is-n't too up-set He'll

fill-the emp-ty cage With an-o-ther lit-tle bird— or two? . . . . (CUN.) He'll
mar-ry Ju-li-ette, And a-dore her for a month— or two! . . . . (WUN-HI.) Me

vow that the ce - re - mo - ny must go on— With some lit - tle girl or
think that he'll break - ee break - ee Wun - Hi's head Some bad luck - ee day or

o - - - ther! And I fan - cy he'll ad - mit That he
o - - - ther! If no beat - ee me with stick, Then he

does - n't mind a bit; For one of them is ve - - ry like an -
giv - ee me a kick— But one of them is well - ee like an -

- o - ther! For one of them is ve - - ry like an - - o - ther!
- o - ther! But one of them is well - ee like an - - o - ther!

MIMOSA.

Oh, what will he do, and what will he say?—Will his lan-guage be im-proper In a

WUN-HI.

Oh, what will he do, and what will he say?—Will his lan-guage be im-proper In a

FAIRFAX.

Oh, what will he do, and what will he say?—Will his lan-guage be im-proper In a

CUNNINGHAM.

Oh, what will he do, and what will he say?—Will his lan-guage be im-proper In a

Ja-pan-e-sey way? He may do what he likes; he may say what he thinks; But we'll

Ja-pan-e-sey way? He may do what he likes; he may say what he thinks; But we'll

Ja-pan-e-sey way? He may do what he likes; he may say what he thinks; But we'll

Ja-pan-e-sey way? He may do what he likes; he may say what he thinks; But we'll pop a lit_tle stop_per On his jol_ly, jol_ly jinks! Oh

pop a lit_tle stop_per On his jol_ly, jol_ly jinks! He may do what he likes; he may

pop a lit_tle stop_per On his jol_ly, jol_ly jinks! He may do what he likes; he may

pop a lit_tle stop_per On his jol_ly, jol_ly jinks! He may do what he likes; he may

what will he do, and what will he

say what he thinks; But we'll pop a lit_tle stop_per On his jol_ly, jol_ly jinks! He may

say what he thinks; But we'll pop a lit_tle stop_per On his jol_ly, jol_ly jinks! He may

say what he thinks; But we'll pop a lit_tle stop_per On his jol_ly, jol_ly jinks! He may

180

say . . . . he may say what he thinks; But we'll pop a lit_tle stopper On his jol_ly, jol_ly jinks!

do what he likes; he may say what he thinks; But we'll pop a lit_tle stopper On his jol_ly, jol_ly jinks!

do what he likes; he may say what he thinks; But we'll pop a lit_tle stopper On his jol_ly, jol_ly jinks!

do what he likes; he may say what he thinks; But we'll pop a lit_tle stopper On his jol_ly, jol_ly jinks!

D.C

DANCE.

Nº 30. QUARTTETTE — "JOLLY YOUNG JACKS ARE WE."

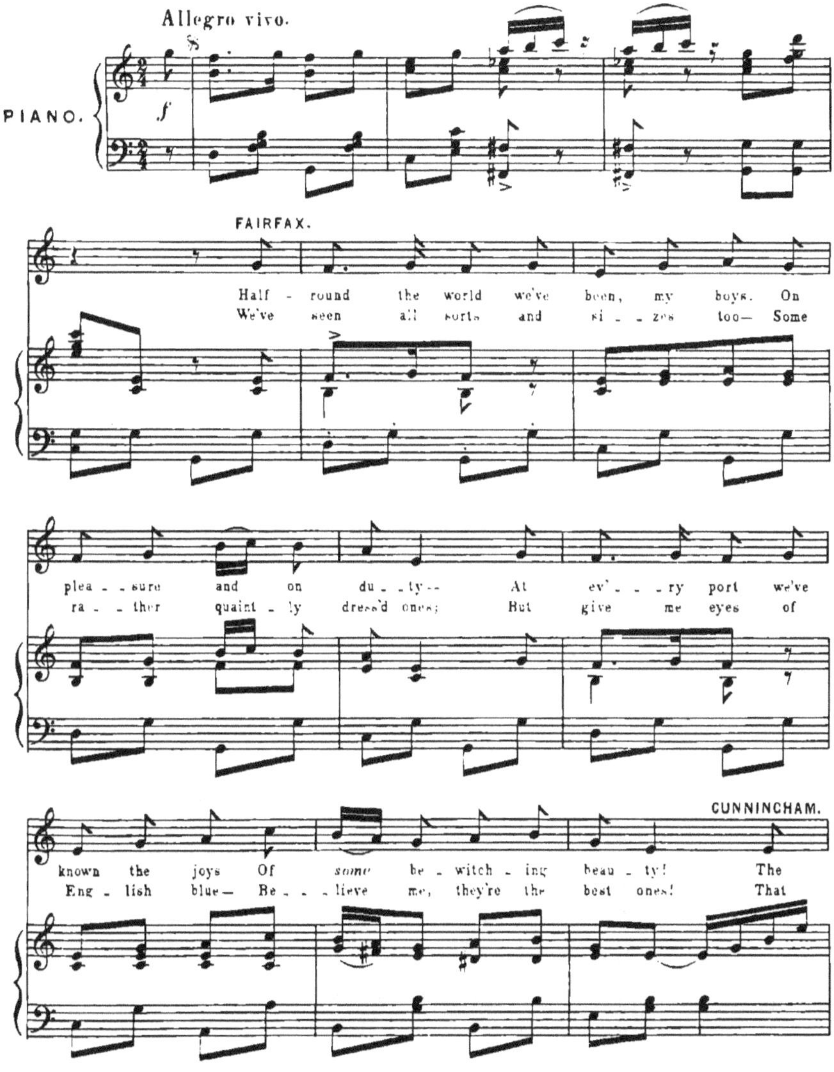

sim - ple maid from sun - ny France, Who blush'd and seem'd to
Chi - nese girl I could - n't stand With feet of small di -
fal - ter The Span - ish girl we met by chance When
- men - sions, Or Gret - chen from the Fa - ther - land, Who
CUDDY.
stroll - ing through Gib - ral - tar. Give me a girl from
ask'd us our in - ten - tions. Well, a - ny you don't
a - ny clime, And I'll a - dore her for a
care a - bout Pass on to me - I'll take them

ALL.
time! out!
Jol_ly young Jacks are we, Mer_ry of heart and gay!–
Sons of the roll_ing sea Homage to Beau_ty pay. What if her eyes are
dark?– What if her eyes are blue?– Beau_ty is fair Ev'_ry_where If
1º Beau_ty's the girl for you! 2º Beau_ty's the girl for you!
D.C.

Jol_ly young Jacks are we, Mer_ry of heart and gay!— Sons of the roll_ing

sea Homage to Beau_ty pay. What if her eyes are dark?—

What if her eyes are blue?— Beauty is fair Ev'_ry_where If Beauty's the girl for

you!

№ 31. SONG— "THE JEWEL OF ASIA."

WRITTEN BY HARRY GREENBANK.

COMPOSED BY JAMES PHILP.

Andante e ben marcato.

1. A small Japanese Once sat at her ease In a gar _ den cool and sha _ _ _ _ _ _ _ _ _ _ dy, When a fo _ reign _ er gay Who was pass _ ing that way Said, "May I come in, young la _ _ _ _ _ _ _ dy?" So she

2. But when he came back (A _ las! and a _ lack!) To that gar _ den cool and sha _ _ _ _ _ _ _ _ _ _ dy, The fo _ reign _ er bold Was de _ _ ci _ ded _ ly cold, And talk'd of an Eng _ lish la _ _ _ _ _ _ dy. With his

By arrangement with Messⁱˢ Willcocks & Cⁱ Ltd.

o _ pen'd her gate, And I blush to re_late That he taught Ja_pan's fair
heart in a whirl For the lit_tle white girl, He de_clared how much he

daugh _ ter To flirt and to kiss Like the lit_tle white Miss Who
miss'd her, And for _ got, if you please, His poor Japan_ese_ For he

lives o'er the west _ _ern wa _ _ter! He call'd her the jew_el of
ne _ _ _ ver... e _ _ ven kiss'd her! But she was the jew_el of

rall:

Delicato.
a tempo.

A _ _ sia, of A _ _ sia, of A _ _ sia, But
A _ _ sia, of A _ _ sia, of A _ _ sia, The

she was the Queen of the Gei _ sha, the Gei _ sha, the Gei _ sha; So she
beau _ ti _ _ ful Queen of the Gei _ sha, the Gei _ sha, the Gei _ sha, And she

laugh'd, "Though you're rea _ dy to _ day, sir, To flirt when I flut _ ter my fan, ... To-
laugh'd "It is just as they say, sir— You love for as long as you can! .... A

mor _ _ row you'll go on your way, sir, For _ get _ ting the girl of Ja _
month, or a week, or a day, sir, Will do for a girl of Ja _

_pan!"
_pan!"

Nº 32. SONG—"I CAN'T REFRAIN FROM LAUGHING."

MUSIC BY **NAPOLÉON LAMPELET.**

I can't re_frain from laugh _ ing for I'm tickled by their plan   Ha! Ha! Ha! Ha! Ha!
Now marriage is   a   mat _ ter far too se _ ri_ous for chaff   Ha! Ha! Ha! Ha! Ha!

Ha! Ha! Ha! Ha! Ha! Ha! Ha! A Gei_sha's much too
Ha! Ha! Ha! Ha! Ha! Ha! Ha! And yet it's so a_
cle_ver for a no_ble of Ja_pan And if they are suc_
_mus_ing that it on_ly makes me laugh I'm long_ing to be
rall:
_cess_ful, they'll be a_ble then to boast
mar_ried in the O_ri_ent_al mode
a tempo.
With par_don_a_ble glee
Yet when I stand be_side
mf

Wher _ e _ ver they may be   How neat _ ly they have
My charm_ing lit _ tle bride   Of course I shall be

(laughing.)

got this haugh_ty gen _ tle _ man on toast!   Ha! Ha! Ha! Ha! Ha!
hap_py, but I know I shall ex _ plode   Ha! Ha! Ha! Ha! Ha!

Ha! Ha! Ha! Ha! Ha! Ha! Ha! Ha! Ha!
Ha! Ha! Ha! Ha! Ha! Ha! Ha! Ha! Ha!

REFRAIN.

Ha! .... I'm tic_kled by a tri_fle it is

true, true, true,   A   fun _ ny lit _ tle fail _ ing I have

riten:

got.   I   can _ not   see   a   joke that o _ thers

do,   do,   do,   And   of _ ten laugh at some _ thing I should

riten:

not. . . . .   Ha!   Ha! Ha! Ha! Ha! Ha! Ha! Ha! Ha!

a tempo.

Ha! Ha! Ha! And of_ten laugh at some_thing I should
cresc:
not . . . . It does_n't mat_ter what, Oh, it
affrettando.
does_n't mat_ter what! Ha! Ha! Ha! Ha! Ha! Ha! Ha!
Ha! Ha! Ha! Ha! Ha! Ha! Ha! Ha! Ha!
rall:
a tempo.
D.C

Nᵒ 33. SONG—"THE WEDDING."

WORDS BY ADRIAN ROSS.

MUSIC BY SIDNEY JONES.

For
At
When
is _ _ n't a time to tar _ ry. . . . . . .
man _ _ _ _ ner phil _ _ _ an _ thro _ pic. . . . . . .
sil _ _ ly young Bri _ _ _ tish tar kiss. . . . . .
all the best of West and of East Is spread on the day I
pre _ sent I must de _ cline. . dis _ pute On the mar _ _ riage pro _ blem
she can mar_ry a belt _ _ _ ed Earl Or a most mag _ ni _ fi _ _ cent

mar _ ry . . . . .
to _ pic . . . . .
"Mar_kiss" . . . .

So
I
She

Is spread for the day I mar _ ry . . . . .
The mar _ _ _ riage pro _ _ blem to _ pic . . . . .
A most mag _ ni _ fi _ _ cent "Mar_kiss" . . .

Is spread for the day I mar _ ry . . . . .
The mar _ _ _ riage pro _ _ blem to _ pic . . . .
A most mag _ ni _ fi _ _ cent "Mar_kiss" . . . .

Is spread for the day I mar _ ry . . . . .
The mar _ _ _ riage pro _ _ blem to _ pic . . . . .
A most mag _ ni _ fi _ _ cent "Mar_kiss" . . . .

Is spread for the day I mar _ ry . . . . .
The mar _ _ _ riage pro _ _ blem to _ pic . . . .
A most mag _ ni _ fi _ _ cent "Mar_kiss" . . . .

fol _ low me in and lift the latch, And drink good health to the
grant ex _ pe _ ri _ ence may have shown, That tak _ _ ing one wife and
may be skit_tish and make a scene, But I shall smile in a

pre _ _ sent match, And clear the board with a hap _ py des _ patch, That
one a lone Is ve _ _ _ ry well in the tem _ pe _ rate zone, But
style se _ rene, And she will be as the rest have been, As

is n't a har _ _ i kar _ i. . . .
I am a tri _ _ fle tro pic . . .
willing as a _ _ ny Barkis . . .

Then
From
For

That is _ n't a har _ i _ kar _ i. . . .
But he is a tri _ fle tro _ pic . . .
As willing as a _ ny Barkis. . . .

That is _ n't a har _ i _ kar _ i. . . .
But he is a tri _ fle tro _ pic . . .
As willing as a _ ny Barkis. . . .

That is _ n't a har _ i _ kar _ i. . . .
But he is a tri _ fle tro pic . . .
As willing as a _ ny Barkis. . . .

That is _ n't a har _ i _ kar _ i. . . .
But he is a tri _ fle tro _ pic . . .
As willing as a _ ny Barkis. . . .

merri_ly pour a glass of champagne, I've tried it be_fore, I'll try it a_gain, I'll
hav_ing one more why should I re_frain, I've done it be_fore, I'll do it a_gain, I'll
when I a_dore_it is not in vain, I've been there be_fore, I'm go_ing a_gain, I'm

try it   as di_et,
do it   go thro' it,
go_ing   so knowing,

He'll try it   as di_et he's tried it be_fore, And he'll try it again and he'll
He'll do it   go thro' it he's done it be_fore, And he'll do it again and he'll
He's go_ing   so knowing he's been there be_fore, And he's go_ing again and he's

He'll try it   as di_et he's tried it be_fore, And he'll try it again and he'll
He'll do it   go thro' it he's done it be_fore, And he'll do it again and he'll
He's go_ing   so knowing he's been there be_fore, And he's go_ing again and he's

He'll try it   as di_et he's tried it be_fore, And he'll try it again and he'll
He'll do it   go thro' it he's done it be_fore, And he'll do it again and he'll
He's go_ing   so knowing he's been there be_fore, And he's go_ing again and he's

He'll try it   as di_et he's tried it be_fore, And he'll try it again and he'll
He'll do it   go thro' it he's done it be_fore, And he'll do it again and he'll
He's go_ing   so knowing he's been there be_fore, And he's go_ing again and he's

198

I'll try it   I'll try it a _ gain....
I'll do it   I'll do it a _ gain....
I'm go_ing   I'm go_ing a _ gain....   **2.** Per _
                                3. For

try it   He'll try it   a _ gain....
do it   He'll do it   a _ gain....
go_ing   He's go_ing   a _ gain....

try it   He'll try it   a _ gain....
do it   He'll do it   a _ gain....
go_ing   He's go_ing   a _ gain....

try it   He'll try it   a _ gain....
do it   He'll do it   a _ gain....
go_ing   He's go_ing   a _ gain....

try it   He'll try it   a _ gain....
do it   He'll do it   a _ gain....
go_ing   He's go_ing   a _ gain....

3rd time.

DANCE.

IMARI.

I'm go_ing, I'm go_ing, I'm go_ing a_gain.

Nº 34. SONG — "MOLLY MINE."

WORDS BY
ADRIAN ROSS.

MUSIC BY
SIDNEY JONES.

Here a-mong the flow-ers, Mol-ly mine,
You dis-trust-ed me girl, Mol-ly mine,

Min-utes go like hours. shade or shine;
Turned a mim-ic-ted girl, Fair and fine:

By the golden gra-ting Where you pine,
Now, too late the dan-ger You di-vine.

I - die I am wait-ing Mol-ly mine.
Cap-tured by a stran-ger Mol-ly mine.

a tempo
Mol-ly, Mol-ly I have strayed in fol-ly,
Mol-ly, Mol-ly play'd with like a dol-ly,

Far from you my dar-ling true and left you wait-ing here;
Just a toy to be the joy of one you hate and fear;

Ah for - get and par - don,
That you shall be nev - er,

Make my heart the gar - den,
Mine you are for ev - er,

Where there blows my Eng - lish rose, my Molly Molly dear.
True and tried my Eng - lish bride, my

Mol - ly Mol - ly dear,

Fine.

No. 35. SONG — (IMARI & CHORUS.) "IT'S COMING OFF TO-DAY."

Oh, I'm long - ing to be mar - ried, For a
When the ce - re - mo - ny's end - ed, The at -
I am go - ing to the mar - riage In a

ba - che - lor I've tar - ried Ra - ther long — the la - dies say; Ve - ry
- trac-tions will be splen-did For the folks who care to stay; Quite re -
new - ly - paint - ed car - riage, And the band of course will play; The de -

of_ten they've re_gret_ted That I was_n't to be net_ted— But at last they've got their
_gardless of the prices, There'll be straw_ber_ries and i _ ces From the shop a _ cross the
_mand so ve _ ry large is That they're put_ting up the charges For the win_dows on the

way! Yet I shan't re_gret my ac_tion If the bride gives sa_tis_fac_tion, And if
way! But if a _ ny _ bo _ dy present Ut _ ters a _ ny_thing un_pleasant Of the
way. I've some tenants in pos_session On the route of the pro_cession, But a

not _ she need_n't stay; But she's dain_ty and de _ li _ cious, So the
bride and bridegroom gay, I may just as well re_mind him That he
week_ly rent they pay; So in spite of all their shin_dies, As I

wedding seems aus_pi_cious, And it's coming off to _ day! To _ day! To _
leaves his head behind him— For it's coming off to _ day! To _ day! To _
want to let their windies, They are coming out to _ day! To _ day! To _

- day! To - day! To - day! In spite of long de - lay, Ma-tri-
- day! To - day! To - day! The pe - nal-ty he'll pay! If to
- day! To - day! To - day! I'll make the peo-ple pay For a

_mo _ ni _ al en-deavour Will be bet-ter late than ne-ver, And it's com - ing off to -
laugh at me he chooses,Then his head at once he lo-ses, For it's com - ing off to -
place of ob_ser-vation At my jol - ly ju - bi - la-tion,Which is com - ing off to -

- day! To - day! to - day! In spite of long de - lay, Ma-tri-
- day! To - day! to - day! The pe - nal-ty he'll pay, If to
- day! To - day! to - day! I'll make the peo-ple pay For a

SOP. 1 & 2.

To - day! to - day! In spite of long de - lay, Ma-tri-
To - day! to - day! The pe - nal-ty he'll pay, If to
To - day! to - day! I'll make the peo-ple pay For a

TENOR.

To - day! to - day! In spite of long de - lay, Ma-tri-
To - day! to - day! The pe - nal-ty he'll pay, If to
To - day! to - day! I'll make the peo-ple pay For a

BASS.

To - day! to - day! In spite of long de - lay, Ma-tri-
To - day! to - day! The pe - nal-ty he'll pay, If to
To - day! to - day! I'll make the peo-ple pay For a

1st & 2nd.

_ mo _ ni _ al endeavour Will be bet_ter late than never, And it's coming off to - day!
laugh at him he chooses, Then his head at once he loses, For it's coming off to - day!
place of ob_servation At my jol-ly ju-bi-lation Which is coming off to - day!

_ mo _ ni _ al endeavour Will be bet-ter late than never, And it's coming off to - day!
laugh at him he chooses, Then his head at once he loses, For it's coming off to - day!
place of ob_servation At his jol-ly ju-bi-lation Which is coming off to - day!

_ mo _ ni _ al endeavour Will be bet-ter late than never, And it's coming off to - day!
laugh at him he chooses, Then his head at once he loses, For it's coming off to - day!
place of ob_servation At his jol-ly ju-bi-lation Which is coming off to - day!

_ mo _ ni _ al endeavour Will be bet-ter late than never, And it's coming off to - day!
laugh at him he chooses, Then his head at once he loses, For it's coming off to - day!
place of ob_servation At his jol-ly ju-bi-lation Which is coming off to - day!

1st & 2nd.

ff

3rd time.
DANCE. (after last verse.)

D.C.

f

mf

Fine.

*9 7 8 3 3 3 7 1 7 2 2 6 8 *